D1510870

REINVENTING THE WHEEL

Marx, Durkheim and Comparative Criminology

Ni He

Austin & Winfield, Publishers
Lanham • New York • Oxford

Copyright © 1999 by
Ni He

Austin & Winfield, Publishers
4720 Boston Way
Lanham, Maryland 20706

12 Hid's Copse Rd.
Cumnor Hill, Oxford OX2 9JJ

Library of Congress Cataloging-in-Publication Data

He, Ni.
Reinventing the wheel : Marx, Durkheim, and comparative
criminology / Ni He.
p.   cm.
Includes bibliographical references.
1. Criminology. 2. Marx, Karl, 1818-1883—Contributions in
criminology. 3. Durkheim, Emile, 1858-1917—Contributions in
criminology. I. Title.
HV6018.H4 1999   364—dc21   99—24373 CIP

ISBN 1-57292-146-3 (cloth: alk. ppr.)

Editorial Inquiries:
Austin & Winfield, Publishers
4720 Boston Way
Lanham, Md. 20706
(301) 459-3366
Website: www.univpress.com
To Order: (800) 462-6420

This book is dedicated to my wife Bing and my son James (Mumu)

Contents

List of Figures

List of Tables

Acknowledgments

My most sincere thanks go to my mentors at the University of Nebraska at Omaha:

Drs. Ineke and Chris Marshall: for their splendid support, personal encouragement and friendship throughout my graduate career in Omaha. Their confidence in me has made all the differences.

Dr. Finn Esbensen: for showing me how to become a disciplined researcher who is well grounded in both theory and methodology. I must say I benefit greatly from those quantitative analysis workshops he sent me to.

Dr. Denn Roncek: for polishing my quantitative skills and teaching me to aim high. I have not forgotten the rules of calculus he once taught me.

Dr. Peter Suzuki: for his fine scholarship and for showing me what a truly caring human being he is.

Grateful acknowledgment is made to the entire Criminal Justice faculty at the University of Nebraska at Omaha for providing the most favorable environment for my doctoral study. My special thanks go to Dr. Jihong Zhao, a dedicated and talented scholar from whom I have learned so much.

I would also like to express my thanks and appreciation to my colleagues at the University of Texas at San Antonio (UTSA) for their encouragements and continuous support: Dr. Derral Cheatwood, Dr. Jim Calder, Dr. Milo Colton, Dr. Mike Gilbert, Dr. Patti Harris, Dr. Becky Petersen, and Judge Steve Russell. I also thank Dr. Dwight Henderson, the Dean of the College of Social and Behavioral Sciences at UTSA, for granting me a course release during the Spring semester of 1999 to focus on this project.

With an enormous sense of gratitude, I wish to express my thanks to Dr. Richard Bennett at the American University who sent me his own copy of the Correlates of Crime (COC) data file through mail. I greatly appreciate his advises and encouragement. I also received help from Dr. Jim Lynch at the American University, Dr. Jim Inverarity at the Western Washington University and Dr. Chris Dunn at ICPSR, University of Michigan.

I owe an apology for being delinquent in delivering the conference papers I have presented to the American Society of Criminology (ASC) annual conferences during the past two years to those who requested them. Many of the materials in those papers are now included in this single work. I hope I can make it up to them by presenting this book in its entirely.

Lastly, I would like to thank Dr. Robert West, Editor in Chief and Ms. Ginger McNally, Technical Editor at Austin & Winfield, Publishers for their enthusiasm, cooperation and support throughout the entire process.

PREFACE

Cross-national comparisons are frequently used to inform debates about crime and criminal justice policy and to test criminological theories. Currently, there appears to be a surge of interest in comparative criminology among an increasing number of scholars. There is also an urgent call for "internationalizing criminology and criminal justice" (Friday, 1997). The development of the field of comparative criminology, however, has been hampered by two major obstacles: the poverty of comparative crime theory and the seemingly unsurmountable methodological complications.

The theoretical and methodological dilemmas in comparative criminology are seen by some as simple extensions of those found in the study of crime involving a single country, e.g., problems of conceptualization, operationalization, validity and reliability of measurement, sampling, whereas others stress the unique character of the problems encountered by comparative criminologists. Comparative criminology has focused on only a handful of reasonably developed theoretical perspectives , e.g., the Durkheimian-Modernization perspective, the Marxian-World System perspective, the Deterrence perspective and the Ecological-Opportunity perspective. Consequently, comparative criminology is not considered a matured and theoretically sophisticated field (Evans et al., 1996:16). To the contrary, comparative research in general and comparative crime theories in particular are charged with embodying an "ethnocentric bias" (Clinard and Abbott, 1973; Shelley, 1985; Neuman and Berger, 1988), and the field is regarded as full of "ambiguity, confusion and misuse of the term 'comparative'" (Blazicek and Janeksela, 1978:34; Beirne, 1983; Birkbeck, 1985; Newman, 1976; Szabo, 1975; Neuman and Berger, 1988:281).

A recent review of the development of comparative criminology reveals that there is little systematic theoretical development in comparative criminology and the existing literature is mostly descriptive and oriented to the pragmatic rather than theoretical (Evans et al., 1996: 15-16). Two possible avenues are envisioned to provide "new" directions in comparative criminology. The first avenue is to "extrapolate from existing theories" to explain crime cross-nationally, e.g., Gottfredson and Hirschi's general theory of crime and Coleman's theory of white-collar crime are presented as examples of theoretical frameworks with potential comparative application. The second avenue is to integrate different theories such as the modernization theory, routine activities theory or anomie theory to explain crime in cross-national context (Evans et al., 1996:22-25).

From a methodological perspective, Bennett and Basiotis (1991:267) argue that the cross-national study of crime is "severely hampered by the lack of centralized, reliable, and valid data sets" and the most current quantitative research often employs limited cross-sectional data sets. Bennett (1991:343) also suggests that the previous research evaluating the adequacy of two popular theoretical perspectives, i.e., the Durkheimian and Opportunity, in cross-national context using cross-sectional designs is flawed. The anomalies and scattered support resulting from testing comparative criminological theories raises doubts of possible mis-specification of the functional form of the theoretical model. In fact, some evidence has been found to suggest that cross-national comparative models should no longer assume only linear relationships but should consider saturation or threshold effects that change or modify the influence of social forces on crime (Bennett, 1991; Bennett and Basiotis, 1991; Unnithan et al., 1994).

Additionally, Neuman and Berger (1988:300) warn that sample selection-the set of nations included in cross-national analysis-may "affect the results far more than has previously been recognized". Therefore, future comparative criminological studies should avoid sample selection bias. Other researchers further recommend that different levels of theoretical explanation be explored with data that simultaneously employ variables at the structural and individual level (Simcha-Facan and Schwartz, 1986).

This book responds to the need for theoretical and methodological advances in cross-national research on crime. My primary purpose is to provide improved empirical testing of the explanatory power of two competing comparative criminological theories--an elaborated Durkheimian-Modernization theory versus a Dynamic Marxian Economic theory of crime. My major goals are to 1) clarify the major theoretical argument of these two competing perspectives in comparative criminology; 2) provide a review of the empirical findings related to the development of these two theoretical perspectives; 3) construct testable theoretical frameworks and hypotheses; 4) apply both cross-sectional and pooled cross-sectional time-series analysis and compare findings based on different samples (i.e., samples involving developed countries and developing countries, separately and combined); and 5) provide theoretical and methodological suggestions for further theory construction and testing.

Plan of the Book

The amount of writing on Marxian theory as well as on Durkheimian theory is enormous. After all, these two men are among the most influential social theorists of the Western world. There is no way that I will be able to summarize and evaluate all of this huge amount of research and theoretical work. Thus, the literature review is limited to the following.

In Chapter I, I provide a brief overview of Marx and Durkheim's views on human nature and society. This will set the stage for the remainder of the review which is divided into two consecutive chapters: Chapter II which introduces the Marxian and Durkheimian writings and research on crime, and Chapter III which focuses on cross-national research and theorizing from Marxian and Durkheimian perspectives. In particular, Chapter II aims to provide a description of the development of Durkheimian and Marxian criminological thought (primarily in the United States and the United Kingdom), including key criticisms, examples of the major empirical studies, as well as more recent theoretical developments. In Chapter III, the Marxian World-System and Durkheimian-Modernization perspectives will be discussed in depth with respect to their explanatory powers in accounting for cross-national differences in criminality.

Chapter IV deals with theory elaboration and modification. This chapter constructs the theoretical framework based on the previous reviews of the Marxian and Durkheimian perspectives on human nature, society and crime. It incorporates past theoretical developments and empirical evidence from both perspectives. It provides separate discussions of the elaborated Durkheimian Modernization and the dynamic Marxian Economic perspectives. The major purpose is to provide testable theoretical frameworks which link the past to the present, and which may contribute to further comparative theory construction and testing.

Chapter V starts with the descriptions of the data sets used for this study. After each of the data sets is separately described, the method of constructing two different data files (cross-sectional and pooled) is introduced, followed by the criteria for sample selection. The subsequent section of the operationalization of variables includes the measurement of the dependent, independent and control variables. Specific hypotheses are formulated based on the theoretical frameworks presented in Chapter IV. Data quality and statistical model specifications, the two key issues in cross-national quantitative studies, are then examined. The final section of this chapter addresses the implications of the discussions on the various methodological issues.

In Chapter VI I present findings from detailed descriptive, bivariate and multivariate analyses using both the cross-sectional as well as the pooled data. Starting with the descriptive statistics, I examine closely the distribution of the data in terms of the means, standard deviations, and the number of valid cases. I provide comparisons of the descriptive statistics between the sub-samples of developed and developing nations. Next, I display the bivariate correlations between each of the dependent variables and the explanatory variables across different time periods. Third, I present findings from three different types of diagnostic tests: (1) the test of sample selection bias; (2) Park's test of heteroskedasticity; and (3) examination of the influential cases using Cook's D, Studentized residual and Studentized deleted residual statistics. Fourth, I present separate discussions of the results from various multivariate regression analyses of both the cross-sectional and the pooled data. Finally, I examine the differences between each of the separate theoretical models and the nested models.

In Chapter VII I conclude this study by focusing on the following: (1) theoretical implications; (2) methodological implications; (3) contributions of this study; (4) limitations of this study; and (5) suggestions for future research. Summary tables are provided when necessary to reflect the most significant findings. Interpretations of these tables are tied to the theoretical hypotheses and results are compared to previous cross-national studies.

It is my sincere hope that this book will revitalize interests in further examining the Marxian and Durkheimian perspectives on crime. I have taken an approach that combines both recent theoretical developments and methodological advancement in the immensely promising field of comparative criminology. I wish I have demonstrated in this book that nation-specific characteristics are essential in understanding crime. Quantitative cross-national studies on crime can benefit greatly from in-depth examinations of the culture and history of nations. This study also illustrates that cross-sectional and pooled analysis can be complimentary to each other if proper care is taken. Methodological issues such as differential case attrition, sample selection bias, influential cases and heteroskedasticity should be carefully addressed. I strongly recommend that diagnostic tests exemplified in this research be systematically used in future quantitative cross-national research.

Chapter I

Marxian and Durkheimian Views on Human Nature and Society

Marx's View

Marx holds a rather holistic social explanation of human nature. He sees human beings as social beings without a precise and fixed nature. The individual's actions, attitudes and beliefs depend on his social relationships and his social relationships depend on his class situation and the economic structure of his society. According to Marx and Engels (1970:42),

> *the mode of production... is a definite form of activity of these individuals, a definite form of expressing their life, a definite mode of life on their part. As individuals express their life, so they are. What they are, therefore, coincides with their production, both with what they produce and how they produce. The nature of individuals thus depends on the material conditions determining their production.*

Marx's view of the social determination of individual behavior contrasts sharply with Hobbes' universal truths about human motivation (Raphael, 1977), Adam Smith's belief that there are certain aspects of a man's make-up which can never be "entirely perverted" (Raphael, 1969) and the assumption of the classical economists that human beings are inherently self-interested. Marx rejects the idea which proposes social conflicts to be the results of the intrinsic competitiveness, aggression and selfishness of man. Marx also declines to accept the Hobbesian approach that "the most can be done towards controlling social conflict is via the agreement to apply sanctions against anti-social behavior" (Campbell, 1981:121).

Instead, Marx believes that man has the potential to be either selfish or unselfish according to the nature of the relationships into which he is born or has to enter. Marx embraces a strong humanistic thought by looking to the full development of man's creative capacities as the ultimate goal of historical progress (Campbell, 1981:116-21). Marx further suggests that communist society is where the spontaneous cooperation between men destroys the alienation between men which leads them to perceive their interests as opposed. Communist society is "the real appropriation of human nature, through and for man. It is therefore the return of man to himself as a social, that is, really human, being" (Bottomore and Rubel, 1961:249).

Marx uses the term "society" in three senses: 1) human society or 'socialized humanity'; 2) historical types of society; and 3) any particular society . Because he regards individuals as social beings, Marx declines to postulate "society" as an abstraction confronting the individual (Bottomore, 1991:504).

Marx's approach in studying the evolution of societies is called historical materialism. Marx views social change on the basis of empirically observable transformations in a society's economic structure (Lynch and Grove, 1986:9). He defines societies by looking at their 'mode of production' (i.e., economic system). The different modes of production include mercantilism, feudalism, capitalism, socialism, and communism, each of which organizes production in a different way. Marx (1954) argues that a society's "mode of production" can be further divided into the "means of production" and the "relations of production". By "means of production", Marx refers to the types of tools and machines, the types of labor, and the types of institutions found in different economic contexts. The "relations of production" is the sociologically most relevant category used by Marx. Marx uses this concept to link any person or group of persons to the means of production in question. By doing so, Marx could make a statement about the group's class affiliation (Lynch and Grove, 1986:9). Marx argues that to understand the historical specific features of any society, we must see both its mode and means of production.

In general, Marx's materialistic science of society is seen as more of a political economy kind rather than sociology (Korsch, 1967). Marx saw class conflict as an essential and economically grounded concept. On the one hand, class divisions resemble the economic divisions. However, the Marxian viewpoint of class divisions should never be equated to the levels of income. Rather, it should be seen as reflecting the antagonistic characteristics of the conflicting economic interests (Campbell, 1981:124). According to Marx (1982:20-1),

> *the economic structure of society is the real foundation, on which rise legal and political superstructures and to which correspond definite forms of social consciousness. The mode of production in material life determines the general character of the social, political, and spiritual process of life. It is not the consciousness of men that determines their existence, but, on the contrary, their social existence determines their consciousness.*

Marx suggests that any economic system will tend to be supported by "superstructures" such as law, politics, education, and consciousness. This also suggests that the superstructure will tend to legitimate both the class structure and the dominant set of economic relationships underpinning it. According to Sykes (1974), Marx has provided us with the notion that one can begin to study a specific society by first looking at the way it is structured economically (i.e., mode and means of production). Next, one should shift one's attention to the relations of production, the aim being to define ways in which different social classes are related to the system of production in question (Lynch & Grove, 1986:12-13).

Marx argued that capitalist societies would inevitably tend to polarize into two groups, one growing smaller and smaller while getting richer and richer, and the other growing larger and larger while getting poorer and poorer. The tendency toward polarization is called "contradiction" in capitalism, and as it became more extreme, it would act as a greater hindrance to the further development of the material forces of production. A revolutionary restructuring of the social relations of production would be inevitable at some point. Socialist collective ownership of the means of production and instituting centralized planning will end the cycles of over-protection and depression that plague capitalism (Vold and Bernard, 1986:302).

Durkheim's View

For Durkheim, the individual is only a residual category in which he places only what is left after he has taken away all that is contributed to human life by society. In general, Durkheim argues that the observable qualities of human beings are not the explanation for or origin of social organization but that social life is both the cause and the end of these apparently individual attributes. For example, in the sphere of moral choice, individuals do not generate moral standards and develop moral commitments. On the contrary, individual values and moral allegiances are the expressions of collective forces which have both a social origin and social function, i.e., to sustain the ongoing social group in which the individuals are located (Campbell, 1981:147-49).

In Durkheim's view, when the moral forces of social life become disintegrated individuals are likely to be left with no idea of what to aim for or how to live a satisfactory life. Anomie, a human condition marked by the absence of social regulation, occurs as a result. "Anomie is thus both a condition of society in which religion, government and morality have lost their effectiveness and the resulting psychological state of disenchanted individuals with no purpose in life and hence no permanent fulfillment" (Campbell, 1981:149).

One of the most distinctive characteristics of Durkheim's assumption of human nature is his social deterministic argument that human appetites have no natural limitation and are naturally insatiable (Durkheim, 1951, [1897]; 1984,

[1893]). Unlike animals which are governed largely by instinct and have relatively fixed and determinate appetites and normally available means to satisfy them, humans have no such inner regulation. According to Durkheim (1951), human life is one of unabated desire resulting in the "malady of infinite aspiration". He wrote in *Suicide* (1951:256, [1897]) that:

> *greed is aroused without knowing where to find ultimate foothold. Nothing can calm it, since its goal is far beyond all it can attain. Reality seems valueless by comparison with the dreams of fevered imagination. Reality is therefore abandoned, but so too is possibility abandoned when it in turn becomes reality. A thirst arises for novelties, unfamiliar pleasures, nameless sensations, all of which lose their savour once known.*

At one point, Durkheim's view of "anomic man" seems to resemble the hedonistic, competitive human nature point of view held by Hobbes. Durkheim, however, sees the remnants of rationality in human life not as the input of human nature as Hobbes would argue but it comes from the residual effectiveness of such social forces as remain operative (Campbell, 1981:150).

Durkheim commented on Marx's theory of society on several occasions (1893; 1928). He recognized as a particular merit of the Marxist theory that it set out to explain social life 'not by the notions of those who participate in it, but by more profound causes not perceived by consciousness' (Durkheim, 1897:648). Durkheim, however, thought that Marxist theory attributed too much importance to economic factors and to class struggles. Durkheim (1893, 1897) argued that class conflict should be seen as a secondary phenomenon arising from the lack of regulation of the new kind of industrial society and he was opposed to the Marxist concept of the state as the "intelligence" and moral agent of society as a whole (Durkheim, 1950).

A society, for Durkheim, is a bounded unit. The boundary, however, is not geographical but moral. The conception of society as a moral phenomenon exemplifies Durkheim's view that "social facts" are external to the individual and constrain their behaviors (Taylor et al., 1973; Campbell, 1981). Durkheim 's sociological positivist approach prompts him to search for the cause of all social phenomena entirely in other social phenomena without any reference to pre-social elements of human nature. He argues strongly that genuine sociology should not include facts that are reducible to any lower degree of reality such as those studied in biology or psychology (Durkheim, 1982, [1895]).

In Durkheim's view, two concepts are crucial to depict social reality: "collective consciousness" and "collective representations". Collective representations are symbols which give meaning for all members of a social group and enable them to identify with each other as group members. Collective consciousness not only embodies all that is included in collective representations, it also entails all ideas which individual members of societies have in common and which stand for collective ends or purposes (Durkheim, 1964).

In *The Division of Labor*, Durkheim (1984, [1893]) differentiates two types of society--the simple and the complex and two associated forms of social solidarity--the mechanical and the organic. A simple, mechanical society is a system constituted by homogeneous segments. Complex societies, on the other hand, are those with large territories, densely populated and include a multiplicity of differently structured groups. In a simple society, individuals are born into clearly defined and tightly integrated social institutions, e.g., family, religious, moral. In complex, organic societies, the familial, religious, educational, political and economic institutions become more distinct and they allow for specialization of roles and significant differences between the individuals who occupy them.

Chapter II

Marxian and Durkheimian Perspectives on Crime

Marxian/Neo-Marxian Perspectives on Crime

Early Marxian Perspectives on Crime (before the 1920s)

Marx did not discuss the problem of crime or its relation to the economic system at length, although he did address the subject in several passages (See discussions of Marx's view of crime in Taylor et al., 1973:209-36 and Beirne and Messerschmidt, 1995). Hirst (1975:215-21) argues that Marx's idea of crime centered on the concept of demoralization. Marx believed that it was essential to human nature that people be productive in life and in work. But in industrialized capitalist societies there are large numbers of unemployed and underemployed people. Because they are unproductive, people become demoralized and are subject to all forms of crime and vice. Marx called these people the lumpenproletariat.

Marx argued against the classical philosophy which held that all people freely and equally joined in a social contract for the common good, and that the law represented a consensus of the general will. Marx maintained that unequal distribution of wealth in a society produced an unequal distribution of power. Marx did not see crime as the willful violation of the common good, but as the "struggle of the isolated individual against the prevailing conditions" (Marx and Engels, 1965:365-67).

Several themes appear in Marxist writing on crime. First, crime is analyzed as the product of class society. In *The Condition of the Working Class*, Engels (1844) argued that the degradation of English workers brought about by the extension of factory production deprived them of volition and led inexorably to crime. Poverty provided the motivation, and the deterioration of family life interfered with the proper moral education of children (Greenberg, 1991:116).

In other writings (e.g., *Outlines of a Critique of Political Economy*, *Speech at Elberfeld, Anti-Duhring*), Engels attributed crime to the competitiveness of bourgeois society which gave rise not only to the crimes committed by impoverished workers but also to fraud and other deceptive business practices (Greenberg, 1991:116).

Both Engels (1973, 1978, 1981, 1983) and Bonger (1916) argue that individual manifestations of criminal behavior are a direct reflection of the strain associated with life under capitalism. Engels' first argument is that every technological advancement associated with capitalist production frees workers from production, generating a larger unemployed population. Engels' second argument is that capitalism generates certain drives such as competitiveness which are both beneficial and harmful to society. Competition benefits capitalists by keeping wages low and productivity high, but it destroys the working class. The working class has to compete not only with the capitalist over working conditions, but also is forced to compete with each other for a limited number of jobs and a limited livelihood. Engels views crime as the result of competition over scarce resources, and sees competition engendered by capitalism as the cause of crime by the masses (1964:224; 1973:168-73), the business classes (1964: 201-02) and middle classes (Engels, 1981:49).

Bonger (1969[1916]) offered the first systematic application of Marxism to the etiology of crime which hypothesized that crime is produced by the capitalist organization of society by which one's class position in society is defined by one's relationship to the means of production (Akers, 1997). Bonger (1916) makes an argument similar to Engels that the competitiveness created by capitalism becomes manifest in individuals as egoism which generates crime among all classes. He provides an extensive theory of crime by arguing that the capitalist economic system encourages all people to be greedy and selfish and to pursue their own benefits without regard for the welfare of others. The political strength of the ruling class enabled it to perform exploitive acts without having those acts treated as criminal behavior. This explains why more lower class individuals are processed by the criminal justice system.

More Recent Developments in Marxian/Radical Perspectives:

After the mid-1920s, Marxist criminology disappeared from the scene in the English-speaking world (Greenberg, 1981:1). Bonger's theory received little acceptance when it first appeared. Non-Marxist class analysis predominated, and economic factors were seen as just one set among a large number of causes of crime (Akers, 1997:169). Mainstream sociological theory of class and crime, e.g., anomie theory, prevailed over Marxist class analysis. In the 1970s, some conflict theorists, e.g., Quinney, Chambliss, Seidman, Platt, Takagi, and Herman and Julia Schwendinger, in the United States started to shift their focus toward a Marxist perspective and rejected their earlier conflict approach (Akers, 1997:161). Two new versions appeared around 1970, one in the US, which developed from conflict theory and was exemplified in the works of Richard Quinney (1980), and the other in Great Britain, which developed from the social reaction perspective and was exemplified in the works of Taylor et al. (1973, 1975).

Taylor et al. (1973, 1975) argued that crime is one significant consequence of the exploitation and oppression of the working class under capitalism. Taylor et al. (1973, 1975) argue that there can be no purely Marxist theory of crime since Marx did not write much about criminal behavior. Since Marxists concentrate on criminal law and the criminal justice system, they have less to say about the causes of criminal behavior. Nevertheless, Taylor et al. (1973:270) do suggest that models of crime causation in the Marxist tradition must include a macro-level analysis which incorporates a political economy of crime. Central to their argument are ways in which crime is affected by the "overall social context of inequalities of power, wealth and authority in the developed industrial society". Further, Taylor et al. (1973:271) suggest that the wider arena of political economy will condition more immediate social milieus, and that these two levels together cause crime.

Quinney (1980) upheld the same view of crime as an inevitable response to the material conditions of capitalism where most proletariat lawbreakers are motivated to commit crimes of "accommodation". According to Quinney (1980:39), the study of crime involves an investigation of such natural products and contradictions of capitalism as alienation, inequality, poverty, unemployment, spiritual malaise, and the economic crisis of the capitalist state. Crimes of accommodation are predatory crimes such as burglary and robbery, which "reproduce" the capitalist system of acquisition of property by expropriating the income and property of others. Violent crimes, such as murder, assault, and rape are also crimes of accommodation committed by those who have been "brutalized" by the capitalist system. He interprets Marx's writing which holds that social production is the primary process of all social life. For Quinney, it is the economic structure which provides a grounding for social and political institutions, for everyday life, and for social consciousness. Deriving directly from Marx's dialectical method which treats the world as a complex of processes in which all things go through a continuous process of coming into being and passing away, Quinney (1980:39) suggests studying all things, including crime, in the context of their historical development, their actual interconnection, contradiction, and movement.

Quinney (1980:41) argues that we should give attention to the following interrelated processes: 1) the development of capitalist political economy, including the nature of the forces and relations of production, the formulation of the capitalist state, and the class struggle between those who do or those who do not own and control the means of production; 2) the systems of domination and repression established in the development of capitalist class and secured by the capitalist state; 3) the forms of accommodation and resistance to the conditions of capitalism by all people oppressed by capitalism, especially the working class; 4) the relation of the dialectics of domination and accommodation to patterns of crime in capitalist society, producing the crimes of domination and crimes of accommodation.

Greenberg (1981) presented a class-based theory of delinquency that has some similarities to strain theories of delinquency. Strain theory measures class in terms of the economic or occupational status of the parents, but Greenberg applied the traditional Marxist view that class should be defined in terms of the relationship to the means of production. Juveniles are described as comprising a class of their own. They are excluded from economically productive activity but are required to engage in extensive training for their future productive role (Vold and Bernard, 1986:306).

Marx (1981:52-3) and Engels (1964:224) once suggested that capitalism "creates a demand for crime which is met by the corresponding supply...". Expanding on this theme, Colvin and Pauly (1983) and the Schwendingers (1976) argue that inequality and stratification that accompany capitalism affect educational opportunities which in turn structure individual propensity to crime. Colvin and Pauly (1983) suggest that family socialization patterns may be related to experiences in the workplace. They broaden past causal inquiry and conclude that 1) socialization patterns in both workplace and family settings are distributed along class lines; 2) that these patterns are defined by the relations of production underlying capitalism, and 3) that these differential socialization sequences determine the patterned process of development of both delinquent and non-delinquent behavior (Colvin and Pauly,

1983:525). Other examples of Marxist approaches to crime are Barnett (1981) who analyzes criminal opportunity as it relates to capital accumulation; and Wallace and Humphries (1981) who reinterpreted the criminogenic effects of urbanization and industrialization by placing these processes within a broader Marxist perspective on investment and capital accumulation. Finally, Chambliss (1988) points to a cyclical struggle between capital and labor from which is born an impoverished underclass whose only solution to their situation is the resort to illegal, underground activity.

Based on Marx's views on class conflict, materialism and the dialectic, Lynch and Groves (1986:46) propose four propositions with respect to crime causation. First, capitalism has at its core a conflict between labor and capital, which means that capitalism is one in a long sequence of historical systems based on inequalities between those who own means of production and those who work. Second, through the fundamental structural inequality between labor and capital, society will be stratified into social classes characterized by tremendous differences in wealth, status, power, and authority. Third, these differences constitute variable material conditions of life which offer persons in different social classes vastly different opportunities in terms of life chances and choices. Their fourth and final proposition is that among these class-based opportunities is the chance or choice of becoming criminal.

In their more recent article, Lynch et al. (1994:15-16) call for a reorientation of radical criminology. They argue that a theoretical and empirical reorientation can be accomplished by making Marx's theory of surplus value the cornerstone of radical theory construction. And such a reorientation would create an empirically testable explanation of crime consistent with Marx's world view. Using time-series data, Lynch et al.'s (1994) analysis demonstrates that the rate of surplus value is a statistically significant predictor of the rate of property crimes known, property crime arrests, violent crimes known, violent crime arrests and total index crimes known to police in the U.S. from 1954 to 1974 controlling for the effects of predictor variables identified in earlier research on crime rates; e.g., percent of 14-21 year old minority males, number of police officers per 1,000 population, police expenditure in millions per 100,000 population. The authors further suggest that the relationship between surplus value and crime "needs to be investigated in other eras and in other countries." In addition, Lynch et al. (1994:37) argue that radical criminologists should investigate alternative measures of the rate of surplus value which can better fit the reality of the current capitalism.

Assessment

Along with the more sophisticated developments in the past two and half decades, the Marxian/radical perspective on crime has also received many criticisms. Some criticisms are from radical/Marxist/critical criminologists. Others are voiced by non-Marxist and mainstream criminologists. In general, most of the conceptual refinements resulting from criticism are made by Marxist/critical criminologists, whereas some of the empirical criticism and tests come from non radical, non-critical criminologists. In the following part of the discussion, I highlight a few of the key contentions.

1) The Role of State: Instrumentalist vs. Structuralist

Kasinitz (1983) observes that during the twentieth century, Western industrial societies have been transformed not by revolution as Marx predicted but by the expansion of the modern welfare state. Therefore, the task of many Western neo-Marxists in recent years has been to develop a theoretical framework for analyzing politics in capitalist nations, which has caused some to move far from the orthodox Marxist tradition. Three trends, relevant to the role of the state are analyzed in his article: 1) "instrumentalism", exemplified by the work of G. William Domhoff (1979, 1981), combines Marxian social class analysis with sociological power elite theory and stresses the role that members of the dominant class play in observable administrative posts; 2) the "relative autonomy" theory, as seen in the work of Nicos Poulantzas (1969, 1973), stresses the division of labor between capitalists and administrators while emphasizing the role of the state in supporting the former as a class; and 3) the "full autonomous" approach, emerging primarily through the work of Fred Block (1977, 1981), asserts that state functionaries are independent actors who act in their own interests usually to maintain economic stability and growth. The last view is seen to be the most promising of the three.

Quinney's explanations of law and criminal justice are known as instrumental Marxism. Some of his critics proposed an alternative Structuralist model of Marxism (Hirst, 1975; Spitzer, 1975; Balbus, 1977; Greenberg, 1981; Chambliss and Seidman, 1982; Chambliss, 1988). The major difference between the two is that the structuralists view the political state as having relative autonomy. In the short run, the state may be autonomous, much of the law and the criminal justice system do not automatically mirror the interests of the capitalists. In the long run, however, there is no difference between Instrumentalist and Structural Marxism. Both agree the long-term historical tendency of the legal system is to reflect and protect the interest of the capitalist class and oppress the masses (Lynch and Grove, 1986).

For Structural Marxists, the state is supportive of capitalism rather than of individual capitalists. The state is itself fragmented, it is composed of various competing agencies, each with their own interests (Spitzer, 1980; Jessop, 1982). The state is also seen as a more or less neutral semi-autonomous political force which controls both capital and labor in the long-term interests of the capitalist system and itself (Beirne, 1979; Greenberg, 1981; Chambliss and Seidman, 1982; Henry and Milovanovic, 1996). In addition, working classes in the capitalist state can form effective interest groups and unions that align with agencies of the state to improve their class position (Einstadter and Henry, 1995).

2) Assessment, Refinement and Suggestions From Fellow Marxist/Critical Criminologists

Greenberg (1981:10) concludes that "by the mid 1970s, a specifically Marxian criminology began to take shape." The new and more rigorous Marxist criminology attempts to relate crime to the political economy of particular societies in which they occur, and relies primarily on historical and cross-cultural studies for support, since only in such studies can societies with different political economies be compared (Vold and Bernard, 1986:305).

The early versions of Marxist criminology were criticized by other Marxists as misinterpreting Marx's thought (see in Hirst, 1975; also in Denisoff and McQuarie, 1975:109-19). Block and Chambliss (1981:4-7) criticized the early theories for their simplistic portrayal of the "ruling class" as a unified and monolithic elite; for the argument that enactment and enforcement of laws reflects only the interests of the ruling class; and for the argument that criminal acts are a political response to conditions of oppression and exploitation.

Greenberg (1976:610-21) raised similar criticisms by arguing that these theories ignored studies which showed people's consensus on legal definitions of crime; that underprivileged people are most frequently victims of crime by other underprivileged people, so that they too have an interest in the enforcement of criminal laws; and that it is unrealistic to expect that crime will be eliminated in socialist societies.

Friedrichs (1979:290-331) argues that the effectiveness of a legal order depends largely on the extent to which it is perceived to be legitimate. In situations when a country is in a crisis of legitimacy, i.e., there is an erosion of faith in leaders and in governmental institutions, disillusionment with the basic values etc., there will be a general increase in various types of illegal behavior, including crime, riots and revolutionary activity.

Initially, Marxist criminologists described criminal behavior in terms of "primitive rebellion" against conditions of exploitation and oppression (Hinch, 1983:69-71). This view has now been widely rejected by Marxists, who look for more complex explanations of crime within the context of the Marxist theory of history and of social change. Some explanations have been proposed and have been found to share some similarity to explanations found in more traditional criminological theories except that they link their basic concepts to a broader view of political-economic systems and the historical processes in which those system change (Vold and Bernard, 1986:306).

Lynch and Grove (1986:45-46) summarize three major criticisms of the radical Marxist criminological approach. First, radical Marxist criminologists, like conflict and labeling theorists, have been criticized because they view crime simply as the mirror image of control, thus ruling out questions of causation or succumbing to tautological reasoning where the only cause of crime is law (e.g., Spitzer, 1980:180; Akers, 1980; Quinney, 1970:123). A second criticism of radical Marxist theorists is that they have limited themselves to an oversimplified "unicausal" approach where the only source of crime is capitalism (e.g., Shichor, 1980). The third criticism has argued that avoiding the issue of causation has resulted in a neglect of empirical research among radicals (e.g., Sparks, 1980; Shichor, 1980; Taylor et al., 1975).

Lynch and Grove (1986) contend that they and other radical criminologists have taken the critiques into account and propose explanations of crime that avoid any "oversimplified, unicausal approach where the only source of crime is capitalism." These explanations stress the effects of economic inequality on crime through alienation, family disorganization, parental socialization practices, and other variables from strain and control theory. Vold and Bernard (1986:305-06) agree that the explanation of criminal behavior as simply a reaction to capitalist oppression is "now rejected by Marxists, who look for more complex explanations of crime within the context of the Marxist theory of history and of social change."

Greenberg (1981:18) calls for a modification of the Marxian explanation for crime:

> *Marxists do not deny that social-psychological processes and face-to-face interactions may have some importance for understanding crime and criminal justice, but they try to see these as shaped by larger social structure. And in characterizing these structures, they give particular attention to the organization of economic activity, without neglecting the political and ideological dimensions of society.*

3) Crime in Socialist Societies

Block and Chambliss (1982) related various types of crime to the political-economic systems of societies in which they occur. They held that crime in a society is essentially a rational response to the contradictions. Chambliss' analysis, however, suggests a moving away from the early utopian position that crime would disappear when the social relations of capitalism were replaced by socialism (Vold and Bernard, 1986:309). Greenberg (1981) takes a similar position and states that the persistence of crime in socialist societies should not be considered a refutation of Marxist theories of crime, but rather should be the occasion of Marxist theories linking the particular nature of crime in those societies to their political and economic arrangements.

Vold and Bernard (1986:309) summarize three types of Marxist crime theories to account for the persistence of crime in socialist countries. First, the theory that crime is a "relic" of capitalism in the sense that elements of capitalist and bourgeois consciousness persist among people despite the establishment of socialism. Second, the theory that crime is rooted in the social inequalities and relative deprivation of present socialist societies. Third, the view that crime springs from the social relations of socialism itself, with an entrenched bureaucracy interested in preserving its own privileges and centralized planning resulting in the powerlessness and alienation of workers.

4) Marxist Theory or Conflict Theory?

Colvin and Pauly (1983:521) point out that Marxist/radical criminology and conflict theory share some similarities in their critical posture toward the prevailing social order, but they are distinguishable by their conceptualization of the nature of the social order. First, conflict theory adopts a pluralistic, conflict perspective of society as an aggregate of diverse interest groups competing for power. Second, radical criminology tends to adopt an instrumentalist-Marxian perspective of contemporary society as dominated by a unified, capitalist ruling class.

Vold and Bernard (1986:299-300) argue that in some ways Marxist criminology can be described as a more specific form of general conflict argument. Like conflict criminology, Marxist criminology contains both theories of criminal behavior and theories of the behavior of criminal law. Conflict criminology describes power as the key structural variable in the explanation of crime, Marxist criminology looks behind power, to the political and economic system, for the ultimate explanation. Crime is explained by the specific characteristics of the political and economic systems that exist during particular historical periods.

Akers (1997:164) argues that:

> The greater the extent to which Marxist theory is modified to account for a multiplicity of conflicts and power groups, the closer it becomes a variation on pluralistic conflict theory. Therefore, the Structuralist model represents something of a movement by some Marxist criminologists back toward conflict theory.

5) Crossfire: Criticisms From Non-Marxist/Non-Radical Criminologists and Responses From Marxist/Radical Criminologist

Jensen (1980) argues that the specific factors used in modified Marxist theories to explain crime, such as economic and racial inequality, urban density, industrialization, family, and peers, are exactly the same factors proposed in mainstream, non-Marxist sociological theories. Akers (1997) argues that the more Marxist theory in criminology is modified to incorporate age, gender, socialization, strain, differential opportunity, and social learning patterns, the less it differs from non-Marxist theories. Akers (1997:170) also argues that Quinney's typology of crimes "does not advance their theory much beyond the basic Marxist assertion that crime is caused by capitalism".

Sykes (1974:212) and Klockars (1980:98) both criticized radicals for being too attached to a two-class model that cannot handle the complexities of stratification in a post-industrial society. Lynch and Grove (1986:17) responded to Hirst's (1979) assertion that radical criminologists "distort...Marxist concepts" by arguing that radicals are duty bound to modify Marxist concepts to better fit a post-Marxist reality. According to Lynch and Grove (1986), radical criminologists see political economy and inequality as important contributors to crime causation. Based on the radical perspective, stratification and inequality are in large part due to political end economic factors as these relate to the antagonism between capital and labor, a defining characteristic of capitalism.

Greenberg (1981: 86) and Sparks (1982) both agree that the goal of radical inquiry is to expand and integrate causal levels as well as to examine how micro level variables such as broken homes or defective educational institutions are shaped by larger social structures. Lynch and Grove (1986:48) concur that radical criminologists should attempt to place micro causal explanations in a wider sociopolitical context. By broadening the scope of criminological inquiry to include significant social, political, and economic institutions, radical criminologists can simultaneously expand the arena in which we search for causes of crime.

There are calls for compromise between radical and traditional approaches. Spitzer (1980) suggests that an us vs. them mentality hampers the development of criminology. Greenberg (1981) and Mungham (1980) call for more use of positivistic methods. Sparks (1982) claims that there is no inherent incompatibility between the traditional emphasis on school and family and the radical preference for political economy. Colvin and Pauly (1983:523) observed that "many insightful contributions to radical analysis have already been made by conventional criminology".

In "Crime, Punishment, and the American Dream: Toward a Marxist Integration," Sims (1997:5) argues that Messner and Rosenfeld (1994) have failed to adequately address the contribution of Marxist criminology to their sociological paradigm. She attempts to join the missing link by suggesting that Marxist criminology can explain how social and economic inequalities are a naturally occurring event in the American system of capitalism. Sims (1997:22) further calls for a reconciliation of both conflict and consensus camps in criminology.

6) Is Marxist Crime Theory Empirically Testable?

A key question needs to be answered: Is Marxist theory empirically testable? Akers (1979) argues that much of the so-called Marxist theory is actually "an ideological condemnation of Western democracies and a call for revolutionary action to overthrow them" (Akers, 1997:164). In general, Akers (1997:165) suggests that there is little in Marxist theory of law and criminal justice that is empirically testable. He contends that "to substantiate their theory, Marxist criminologists must make the proper kinds of comparisons between real socialist and real capitalist societies" (Akers, 1997:166). Akers (1997:174) also wrote: "the concept of socialist society as a future utopia that has yet to be established in reality renders Marxist theory untestable".

Empirical test of criminological theory was traditionally regarded as "bourgeois" in nature by radical criminologists. An increasing number of radical criminologists, however, have realized the fallaciousness of the general radical dismissal of empirical observations as a method (e.g., Groves, 1985; Lynch, 1987; Greenberg, 1981). In his assessment of the current state of the radical criminology, Lynch (1996:298) argues that "the division among radical criminologists between die-hard anti-empirical supporters and data-based radicals has distracted attention from the real issues and goals of data-based radical analyses and has created dissension where none should exist." He suggests that radical criminologists can challenge the mainstream assumptions and findings by employing radically oriented variables in empirical tests and pitting these variables against variables representing traditional criminological perspectives (Lynch, 1996:299).

Summary

Following a brief discussion of the early Marxian perspectives on crime (i.e., perspectives mainly from Marx, Engels, and Bonger), I provided a general historical overview of the more recent developments in the vein of Marxist criminology. As mentioned previously, my description of the development of the Marxian criminological thoughts could not possibly be exhaustive. Rather, I focused on a few focal points, and I limited my discussions on those thoughts developed primarily in the U.S. and the U.K.

For the discussion of the recent theoretical developments, I included the thoughts from the following major theorists: Taylor et al. (1973, 1975), Quinney (1980), Greenberg (1981), Colvin and Pauly (1983), Lynch and Groves (1986) and Lynch et al. (1994). I also included the discussion of the following focal points: 1) the role of the state; 2) the assessment, refinement and suggestions from fellow Marxist/Critical criminologists; 3) crime in socialist societies; 4) Marxist theory or conflict theory; and 5) criticisms from non-Marxist, non-radical criminologists.

In conclusion, I find that both theoretical developments and empirical research based on the radical/Marxist criminological perspective remain sparse compared to those in mainstream criminology. However, it is evident that efforts have been made to improve communications between the radical and the mainstream criminologists. When responding to challenges from mainstream criminologists, several radical/Marxists seem to have adjusted their traditional, ideological tone and reacted in a more scientific, nonideological manner. In fact, some of the radical criminologists are among themselves the fiercest critics of the radical/Marxist theory. Some of them have already proposed integrated, modified Marxist theories of crime. Others call for inclusions of more empirical assessments of the radical/Marxist criminology as a new way of communicating with mainstream criminology . It is believed that by doing so, the radical empiricist can make greater headway in altering the mainstream view of crime (Lynch, 1996).

Durkheimian Perspective on Crime

Early Durkheimian Perspective on Crime

Durkheim invested a considerable amount of time and space in discussing crime (Taylor et al., 1973). In *The Division of Labor in Society*, Durkheim (1964:80) defined crime as an act which "offends strong and defined states of the collective conscience". He regarded crime as "the very negation of solidarity" and the criminal as someone who "seeks to live at the expense of society" (Durkheim, 1964:353-54). In *The Rules of the Sociological Method* (1895), Durkheim developed one of his major concepts which defines "crime as normal". In *Suicide* (1897), Durkheim provides an extensive discussion of "anomie"-the other key concept.

1) Crime as Normal

Durkheim (1965) argues that crime is normal in a society. Crime is an inevitable phenomenon of organized society reflecting the diversity of behavior of society. The definition of crime is seen as a labeling process within the existing collective conscience. Crime serves as one type of social control which marks the boundaries of public morality (Durkheim, 1964:68). Societies with too little crime or with too much crime are both pathological. Crime is thus functional; it does not only "open the path to necessary changes", it also directly prepares these changes (Taylor et al., 1973:80). In his own words, Durkheim (1964:72) wrote:

> *crime...must no longer be conceived as an evil that cannot be too much suppressed. There is no occasion for self-congratulation when the crime-rate drops noticeably below the average level, for we may be certain that this apparent progress is associated with some social disorder.*

Durkheim ties his discussions on crime with the development of individualism and the issue of collective conscience. In *The Division of Labor in Society*, Durkheim (1964) defines the concept of collective conscience as the "totality of social likenesses." He argues that in every society, there will always be some degree of diversity which marks the difference between individual members. In a mechanical society which is often characterized by the uniformity of the lives, work and beliefs of its members, social solidarity mainly comes from the pressure for strengthening uniformity against diversity. Among the various forms, the application of criminal sanction is the strongest format utilized to reenforce the sense of collective identity which is the major source of social solidarity. The criminalization of certain deviant behaviors is the price a society pays to remain healthy. Criminals are among the group of those identified by society as inferior, which allows the rest to feel superior. The number of those criminalized should, on the one hand, be large enough to constitute an identifiable group. On the other hand, however, it should not be so large that a substantial portion of the society is involved (Vold and Bernard, 1986).

2) Anomie, Individualism and Crime

For Durkheim, the causes of crime can be summarized to include the combination of the following four sociological aspects: (1) the breakdown of the traditional moral structures; (2) forced division of labor; (3) heightened individualism; and (4) the unsynchronized adaptation of social structure to accommodate rapid social change (Einstadter and Henry, 1995:156).

Unlike the mechanical society where social solidarity is often derived from pressure for conformity through repressive penal sanctions, organic society employs regulatory law to direct diversified social behaviors. When this kind of regulation becomes inadequate, a society is in a state of anomie. Crime and other social maladies occur as a consequence of anomie. In *The Division of Labor in Society*, Durkheim (1965) argues that industrialization with its resulting division of labor can destroy the traditional solidarity based on uniformity in mechanical society. In *Suicide*, Durkheim (1952) maintains that rapid industrialization accompanied by insufficient regulation, e.g., laws, religion, government policy and so on, creates a chronic state of anomie in which individual appetites are no longer curbed. Deviance including suicide as well as various crimes, occurs as the result of such normlessness.

According to Durkheim (1965), the increased division of labor reduces the pervasiveness of the collective conscience in a society. The growth of individualism, as an inevitable consequence of the expansion of the division of labor, progresses at the expense of the strength of common beliefs and sentiments (Giddens, 1971:79). Durkheim perceives the process of development from primitive to advanced society as a transformation of the moral basis from collective conscience to moral individualism (Huang, 1995:66). Like Spencer, Durkheim views the modern individual as a discrete entity or personality who is literally created as an effect of the advanced division of labor. Durkheim (1933), however, envisioned a different kind of individualism what he called "moral individualism" and "cult of the individual". Moral individualism, conceptualized as "the common morality attached to the individual and his interests," depicts the respect of citizens concerning individual freedom, rights and dignity (Durkheim, 1951:356). Moral individualism is also regarded by Durkheim as the cultural correlate of the structural reality of economic specialization (Perrin, 1995:801). Durkheim (1933:407) wrote,

> *We remember that the collective conscience is becoming more and more a cult of the individual, we shall see what characterizes the morality of organized societies, compared to that of segmental societies, is that there is something more human, therefore more rational, about them.*

By treating humanity and rationality as the major concerns of morality in an organized society, Durkheim argues that the ignorance of individuation increases the level of homicide because it fails to form a respect for the rights and dignity of human beings. Durkheim (1951:356) contends that: "whenever society is integrated in such a way that the individuation of its parts is weakly emphasized...no soil is so favorable to the development of the specifically homicidal passions."

3) Durkheim's Influence in the United States Beginning in the 1920s and 1930s

Durkheim's theory has been very influential in the United States. Partially derived from Durkheim's argument that rapid social changes and increasing division of labor are conducive to crime due to the breakdown of social norms and rules, the Chicago School of Human Ecology began to take shape in the 1920s in the US. Representative theorists of the Chicago School are Robert Park (1936), who proposed a parallel between the distribution of plant life in nature and the organization of human life in societies, Ernest Burgess (1928), who argued that cities have a tendency to expand radially from their center in patterns of concentric circles, and Clifford Shaw and Henry McKay (1931, 1942), who studied the problem of juvenile delinquency not from any biological or psychological abnormalities but from a human ecology perspective. For example, included in their analysis are the physical status (location, housing), economic status (income, welfare) and population composition (racial and ethnic) of the neighborhoods where delinquent youth live.

In the late 1930s, Robert Merton (1938) proposed a theoretical interpretation of crime in American society based on his revision of Durkheim's original concept of anomie. Merton (1938) argued that human appetites can be "culturally induced". When the prominent cultural goal such as acquiring wealth exceeds far beyond the rewards, strain is experienced, especially by people of lower social strata.

Durkheim's influence is also prominent in modern control theory of delinquency. In general, it is recognized that varieties of control theories share one particular attribute-they focus on why most people do not commit crimes, rather than why some people do commit crime. The explanation lies largely in the restraining or controlling forces imposed on individuals. The representative control theorists include Albert Reiss (1951), Jackson Toby (1957), F. Ivan Nye (1958), Walter Reckless (1961), David Matza (1964) and Travis Hirschi (1969). Moreover, Vold and Bernard (1986) suggest that Durkheim also provided the theoretical foundations for labeling theory. Such an influence can be traced to Durkheim's (1964:70) own writing about what confers the quality of crime upon acts "is not the intrinsic quality of a given act but that definition which the collective conscience lends them".

Assessment and Criticisms of Durkheimian Perspective on Crime

Because of the enormous amount of work that has been generated throughout the years, my review of the assessment and criticisms of the Durkheimian perspective cannot be exhaustive. I highlight the following because of their significance to the current inquiry: (1) the discussions of Durkheimian theoretical assumptions and their logical coherence; and (2) the examination of the relevant empirical evidence.

1) Discussions on the Theoretical Assumptions and Their Logical Coherence

Lukic (1974) recognizes Durkheim as among the first to elaborate a functionalist conception of the social basis of morality. Durkheim maintains that every society evolves a morality which supports its self-preservation. Even pathological facts, such as crime, are functional. Lukic (1974), however, argues that Durkheim's functionalism is insufficiently precise because one can not decide whether a particular social fact contributes to the self-preservation of a specific society or of society in general. He also argues that there are instances where morality demands society's self-annihilation--suicide. And the manner in which a society creates a functional morality is unexplained. Therefore, morality may be considered functional only in certain epochs and partially.

Kellogg (1977) introduces an analysis linking criminal penalties and social evolution from a Durkheimian perspective. He observes that a new penal philosophy is developing in accordance with principles foreign to Durkheim. Punishment is now tied to the importance of the harm done consciously by the criminal. And the need for coherent sentencing is greater than the need to fit the punishment to the criminal. It is argued that this contemporary evolution had not been anticipated by Durkheim, but is nevertheless a confirmation of his evolutionist theory and the progressive replacement of collective consciousness by moral consciousness.

Roshier (1977) argues against Durkheim's notion that crime is socially functional and inevitable. He contends that Durkheim's argument rests on the confusion of inevitability with necessity. He further suggests that the corrective approach which seeks to eliminate crime from society appears considerably more humane when contrasted to Durkheim's theory of crime as something which society must manufacture and then punish to maintain its own stability.

Jones (1981) argues that Durkheim's followers who deal with crime and punishment have focused on his earlier formulations (e.g., in *The Division of Labor, 1893, The Rules of Sociological Methods, 1893 and Suicide,* 1897) rather than his more adequate later ones, e.g., *Two Laws of Penal Evolution, 1900,* and thus have failed to develop the full theoretical potential of his ideas. Jones (1981:1015) suggests that the major innovation in the "Two Laws of Penal Evolution" was Durkheim's (1900) vision of seeing forms of punishment as dependent not only on the level of social differentiation, but also on the type of political structure. According to Durkheim (1900:285-94), *the law of quantitative change*, the first law, asserts that "the intensity of punishment is the greater the more closely societies approximate a less developed type--and the more the central power assumes an absolute character." *The law of qualitative change*, the second law, maintains that "deprivations of liberty, and of liberty alone, varying in time according to the seriousness of the crime, tend to become more and more the normal means of social control." Jones (1981) proposes that a reformulated Durkheimian model must be developed before further progress can be achieved toward an adequate evolutionary theory.

Machalek and Cohen (1991) challenge Durkheim's thesis that crime is beneficial for society because social solidarity is strengthened when punitive measures are enacted. They argue that Durkheim's logic consists of a reified view of society that leads to "group-selectionist" thinking and a "teleological" account of the causes of crime. Drawing on evolutionary game theory to reconceptualize the relationship between crime and punishment, it is suggested that crime (cheating, within the game-theoretic context) may confer benefits on cooperating individuals by promoting stability in their patterns of cooperation. Machalek and Cohen (1991) conclude that it is not the objective impact of crime on society that signifies its most serious costs, but its implied threat to reciprocity that most seriously threatens society. In a later work, Cohen and Machalek (1994) criticize that Durkheim's theory of crime causation suffers from several serious logical flaws. They argue that, despite his reputation for propagating a purely sociological explanation of crime, Durkheim resorts ultimately to individual characteristics rather than social facts to identify the root causes of crime. They suggest that contemporary evolutionary game theory affords an alternative explanation of the normalcy of much crime without suffering the deficiencies of the classical Durkheimian approach.

Takala (1992) critically assessed the Durkheimian argument that crime is a necessary and even useful component of a healthy society. Linking this argument to

Durkheim's particular understanding of scientific concepts, the role of causality and his standards for distinguishing pathological behavior from normal behavior, Takala (1992) finds Durkheim's doctrine of the utility of crime to be erroneous.

2) Empirical Examinations

Blumstein and Cohen (1973) critically reexamine Durkheim's claim of the existence of stable levels of crime and offer an alternative argument for the stability of punishment. They present a theoretical structure which characterizes deviant behavior and society's responses to it in terms of a multidimensional behavior distribution which can vary over time. A conservation theory is hypothesized suggesting that, first, a fairly constant level of punishment is imposed by society. This level of punishment should vary between societies reflecting consideration of a society's homogeneity and its permissiveness toward deviance. Secondly, the range of behavior that is punished varies with shifts in the behavior distribution, expanding as actual behavior becomes less deviant and contracting as the populace becomes more deviant. Some supporting empirical evidence is provided in the form of imprisonment rates for the United States and Norway and an analysis of changes apparent in arrest data for the United States.

Collette et al. (1979) test the Durkheimian proposition that various forms of deviance reflect both degree and type of social integration in a community. Using data from 18 urban areas in New Zealand, the authors find that urban suicide and alcoholism vary directly with measures of functional integration and inversely with measures of normative integration.

Greenberg (1980) proposed two different explanations for the oscillatory behavior of imprisonment rates in several Western capitalist nations. One of these is based on the Durkheimian model of a collective conscience that responds homeostatically to deviance. The other sees prison populations as changing in response to unemployment. Both explanations are tested with data on crime and imprisonment in twentieth-century Poland. Neither explanation is confirmed.

Greenberg (1980) suggests that the correct explanation appears to lie instead in the political realm.

Schattenberg (1981) compares the practices of social control agencies (mostly bureaucratic organizations) with Durkheim's expectations regarding the role of punishment in society. Durkheim argued that while punishment might have deterrent effects on crime, its main function is the maintenance of social cohesion through the public affirmation of collective moral sentiments. Since the workings of the bureaucratic structures charged with social control involve a low degree of visibility and are highly accommodative, Durkheim's model does not seem to be applicable to modern practice. Schattenberg (1981) argues that the social role Durkheim ascribed to punishment has been transferred to the program content of mass media entertainment, including TV programming.

Chandler (1984) criticizes Messner (1982) for having committed an error in testing a model based on Durkheim's theory of the relation between homicide and societal development. Chandler argues that not only is Messner's (1982) conclusion false, but he created considerable theoretical confusion with regard to the role of moral individualism in a society's bent toward violent crime. The author points out that much of the confusion appears to have arisen because of Messner's reliance on Giddens' (1971) interpretation of Durkheim's thoughts in *The Division of Labor in Society*.

Mestrovic and Alpert (1989) apply Durkheim's concept of anomie to the stock market crash of 1987. They hypothesize that economic anomie produces "sociopsychoorganic" symptoms in United States society as a whole, along with conditions that lead to insider trading, white-collar crime and other crises. The authors suggest that, if verified, this new reading of Durkheim's theory of economic anomie holds the potential for changing the organization of the economic sector of society in order to minimize anomie and thereby minimize future economic crises. Smith and Wong (1989) examine Durkheim's proposition on individualism and crime rate. Their regression analysis of data from 148 SMSAs supports the proposition that individualism leads to lower homicide rates but higher non-homicide crimes.

Kim et al. (1993) test a Durkheimian hypothesis that social solidarity should influence both deviance and its opposite, conformity to social norms. Their confirmatory factor analysis of government statistical data on 116 US metropolitan areas shows that deviance (crime, suicide, divorce, alcoholism and illegitimacy) and conformity to social norms (charity and voter turnout) comprise a single latent dimension. They argue that industrial diversity increases deviance by its indirect effects through mechanical solidarity, organic solidarity and domestic solidarity. Racial diversity increases crime indirectly by diminishing mechanical solidarity, but reduces other deviance by increasing domestic solidarity.

Summary

This section started with a brief introduction of Durkheim's major perspectives relevant to the discussion of crime. These include: (1) Durkheim's argument that crime is normal and functional in a society; and (2) Durkheim's discussions on anomie, individualism and crime. It then provided a short review of Durkheim's influence in the United Stated starting in the 1920s and 1930s.

It seems that, in spite of the gigantic amount of secondary literature, there is surprisingly little integrated work which has tested the full strength of Durkheim's theory. I concur with Jones' (1981:1009) assessment that "the full theoretical potential of Durkheim's idea on crime and punishment has not been developed by his followers, who have focused on his earlier, less defensible formulations at the expense of his later, more significant developments." I argue that further and more comprehensive theoretical exercises are needed before the theory can be tested empirically, and before an objective assessment of the Durkheimian perspective can be made.

Chapter III

Cross-National Applications of Marxian and Durkheimian Perspectives on Crime

Marxian World System Theory (MWS)

Origin and Early Perspectives

In the first paragraph of Volume One, part II, chapter IV of *Capital*, Marx (1978:329) wrote: "the modern history of capital dates from the creation in the 16th century of a world-embracing commerce and a world-embracing market". In the third volume of Capital, Marx (1981) views the competition on the world market as the basis for and a vital element of capitalist production. He makes the creation of the world-market one of the three cardinal facts of capitalist production, on a par with the concentration of means of production in a few hands and the organization of labor itself into social labor (see in *Capital*, Volume Three, part III, chapter 15, section 14). In one of his earlier writings, Marx (1857) also asserted that "the tendency to create the world market is directly given in the concept of capital itself." However, Marx did not give a concrete analysis of how the world market operates in *Capital* (Wallerstein, 1991). Rather, it was the world-system theory of Wallerstein (1974) which provided the explicit link between Marxism and the need to examine societies "as parts of systematic pattern of relations among societies" (Robertson, 1992:13).

According to Wallerstein (1991:591), the reality of world political developments after the Second World War forced back on the Marxist agenda the issue of capitalism as a world-system. A so-called internal/external factor distinction is at the heart of the debate. For some the class struggle internal to the state social formation is primary, and external factors such as world trade are secondary. For others, not only has a trans-national division of labor marked capitalism from its earliest history, but also they find that it is integral to the mode of functioning of capitalism.

Wallerstein (1974) argues that the uneven advance of the global capitalist economy produces a world system that consists of a "core", "periphery", and "semi-periphery". The core refers to those highly industrialized nations with advanced capitalist relations. They receive high profit by extracting raw materials and by taking advantage of the cheap labor market from the periphery. The periphery is composed of those economically dependent Third World countries which have to depend on the core for manufactured goods and cultural products. The economy of the periphery is most likely to be unbalanced because of its debt obligations with the core. The semi-periphery nations are partially industrialized and serve as economic and political "buffers" between the core and the periphery nations. Wallerstein's theory has been used by several social scientists studying crime in a comparative context.

Recent Developments

Emerging since the early 1980s, the dependency paradigm has been used to study the problem of third world crime (Evans and Timberlake, 1980; Bornschier and Chase-Dunn, 1985). According to the dependency perspective, third world crime should not be seen as a direct effect of modernization or development which is the argument held by Durkheimian-Modernization perspective. Rather, it should be viewed as a part of the distinct social formation resulting from its specific position in the world economy and the accompanying capital penetration by the dominant core nations (Chen, 1992:44). For example, Bornschier and Chase-Dunn (1985) argue that the poverty problem in the less developed nations can be a result of the decapitalization process of the economic dependency that is drawing the profit, interests and capital from the dependent nations. And this is seen to be correlated to criminality in the third world countries.

Humphries and Wallace (1980) argue that urban crime is induced by the uneven expansion and contraction of the capitalist production process within and between nations. Patterns of uneven economic activity and employment should explain variation in crime rates within core and between the core and periphery. Walton (1982) suggests that capitalist relations penetrate unevenly within societies that have different social and cultural conditions. He argues that the location of a nation in the world system shapes its class structure, economic conditions, political institutions and social relations which affect crime.

Bush (1983) argues that the demise of the liberal welfare state, increasing unemployment due to plant closures, and the increasing immigration of workers from peripheral zones of the capitalist world economy are all elements of the current crisis in capital accumulation and the changing international division of labor. In general, the Marxian-World System perspective defines crime as a socio-political concept that reflects production and power relations which are intrinsically linked to a society's relation to other societies (Chambliss, 1976; Humphries and Greenberg, 1981; Lopez-Rey, 1970; Sumner, 1982; Neuman and Berger, 1988). This perspective treats industrialization and urbanization as the outcomes of capitalist expansion. Unlike the Durkheimian-Modernization perspective which applies modernization as a key predictor of crime rates (see next section), the Marxian-World System perspective uses modernization only as an intervening variable. The latter perspective argues that the effect of industrialization and modernization depends on how modes of production articulate with one another (Schwendinger and Schwendinger, 1985; Neuman and Berger, 1988).

Neuman and Berger (1988:284) provide a concise review of the Marxian-World System perspective on crime. They describe that the main causal variables in the Marxian-World System perspective are the "global economy and uneven expansion of the capitalist mode of production, the international system of states, class structure and conflict, economic inequality, the class nature of the state, and the spread of new ideologies". They also comment that:

> *the strength of the MWS approach lies in its use of world system and political factors to explain broad patterns of crime (both traditional and nontraditional) within and between nations. However, it is less concerned about criminal behavior per se because it views crime as merely one manifestation of capitalist social relations. Its focus on macro-level historical processes thus limits its ability to explain crime at the level of individual behavior (Neuman and Berger, 1988:300).*

Empirical Assessment and Criticisms

Only a handful of empirical studies have been conducted to test the Marxian World System (MWS) perspective on crime. Humphries and Wallace (1980) examine capitalist accumulation and urban crime in a Marxian World System perspective. Their analyses support the relationship between urban accumulation and crime. It is suggested that urban accumulation shapes industrialization and urbanization which then influence crime rates. Lynch et al. (1988) test the Marxian World System perspective on the crimes of homicide, theft, fraud and robbery in a cross-national sample. They hypothesize that rates of violent and property crime will differ according to world system location. Core nations will have higher rates of property crime because of the democratic and egalitarian ideologies. Periphery countries will have higher rates of violent crime due to political repression, frustration-aggression reactions, and alienation. Using income inequality (Gini index) and energy consumption per capita as control variables, Lynch et al.'s (1988) study finds support for their major hypotheses with regard to crimes in the core and the periphery. The patterns for semi-periphery nations, however, are not clear.

In a content analysis of articles on "crime and development" published between 1960 and 1979 and indexed by the National Criminal Justice Reference Service, Huggins (1985) sums up the following three conclusions: 1) there is a dearth of published research on Third World crime; 2) there is a focus on crime control; and 3) there is a lack of research about crime by and against Third World women. Extant theory and research suggest two models for studying Third World crime. One involves the combination of the traditional theories of criminology with modernization theory's evolutionary assumptions about societal development. The other combines radical theories of criminology with the dependency perspective on development. The "political-economy/dependency" model examines the impact of class-structured inequalities between nations on internal conditions, including local definitions and treatment of crime. Huggins (1985) advocates the increased use of the political-economy/dependency approach.

Horton and Platt (1986) provide a discussion of the advantages and limits of crime control in socialist societies. They argue that mainstream, procapitalist criminologists assume the universality of crime as the inevitable by-product of modernization and attribute the diminution of crime under socialism to totalitarian methods of social control, while radical criminologists generally neglect the study of socialist societies and have often idealistically measured the successes of socialism by a utopian blueprint for national development. They suggest that World-System theory offers a promising, nonmoralistic alternative to both positions by examining the uneven course of socialist constructions within the operation of a single capitalist world economy and unstable interstate system.

In his empirical investigation of cross-national perspectives on female crime, Clark (1989) examines the following three theoretical approaches: Durkheimian Modernization (DM), Marxian World System (MWS) and Ecological Opportunity (EO). Both convergent and divergent hypotheses about female criminality are tested.

The DM and MWS approaches are seen as anticipating direct associations between female labor force participation and female property crime. The DM approach expects associations between per capita gross national product (GNP) and urban share of population and female property crime, while the MWS approach anticipates negative associations between some versions of dependency and female property crime. The EO approach expects an interaction effect among GNP per capita, female labor force participation and urban population on female crime. Using female crime statistics from INTERPOL for 1985/1986, Clark (1989) found no evidence to disprove any of these three theoretical perspectives.

Using a cross-national data set including 61 nations, Simpson and Conklin (1992) tested the hypothesis of the possible effect on national homicide rates of economic penetration by transnational corporations. Such an effect was found to be limited. Simpson and Conklin (1992), however, found that centralized nations have lower expected homicide rates. They suggest that political systems do have a strong influence on national homicide rates even after known demographic correlates of crime are controlled.

Summary and Conclusion

This section discussed the origin, development and empirical examinations of the Marxian World-System perspective. Inspired by Wallerstein's (1974) World-System Theory and the general Marxian perspective on crime, criminologists have been trying to synthesize the two. The Marxian World System perspective defines crime as a socio-political concept that reflects production and power relations which are intrinsically linked to a society's relation to other societies. Empirical analyses have yielded some support to the Marxian World System theory and its variant-the dependency theory. Critics credit the Marxian World System perspective for its application of both world system and political factors to explain broad patterns of crime within and between nations. Meanwhile, it is also recognized that the Marxian World System perspective is less concerned about criminal behavior per se because it views crime as merely one manifestation of capitalist social relations (Neuman and Berger, 1988).

Durkheimian-Modernization Theory (DM)

Major Concepts

Durkheimian-Modernization (DM) theory has been a dominant force in cross-national studies of crime (Neuman and Berger, 1988:281). The DM perspective uses the nation state or society as the unit of analysis. It posits that all nations develop through similar stages. The DM perspective employs key terms such as industrialization, population growth, urbanization, the division of labor, social disorganization, anomie, modern values and cultural heterogeneity in explaining variation in crime rates (Archer and Gartner, 1984; Barberet, 1994; Cohen, 1982; Clinard and Abbott, 1973; Durkheim, 1964; Jones, 1985; Krohn, 1978; Messner, 1982; Shelley, 1981; Toby, 1979; Vold and Bernard, 1986; Huggins, 1985; Neuman and Berger, 1988).

The concept of modernization is applied to analyze the process of societal transformation because of demographic, economic and technological changes. A commonly shared view specifies modernization as the processes of cultural, political and economic development, and as a continuing process of structural differentiation (Heiland and Shelley, 1991:5). While some view technological progress as a decisive stimulus for the modernization of the society (Levy, 1966), others lay more emphasis on social and cultural development in economic or religious areas (Weber, 1920).

From a Durkheimian point of view, urbanization and industrialization can be immediately employed to explain variation in crime rates. First, industrialization changes a society from one characterized by mechanical solidarity with a strong collective conscience and popular use of repressive laws to control deviance (agrarian society), to one characterized by organic solidarity with a complex division of labor and predominant use of restitutive laws to regulate social behaviors (industrial society) (Durkheim, 1964). Crime would occur (as innovation and deviation) when the normative systems fail to keep up with the change in the division of labor. Secondly, urbanization, which often accompanies the industrialization process, weakens familial and community ties and gives one anonymity and frees one from traditional informal social control (Shelley, 1981; Clinard and Abbott, 1973).

Modernization theory posits partially the consequences of the social bonding perspective at the micro level of analysis. Grove et al. (1985:59) state that "as a society becomes more modernized, secularized, urbanized, industrialized, bureaucratized or rationalized, its traditional bonds break down. Although these traditional bonds may be replaced by bonds of a different kind, the developmental process leads inevitably to increased rates of violent crime". Shelley (1981:54-55) suggests that social processes accompanying industrial development have resulted in conditions conducive to increased criminality such as loosened family ties, instability of family and lack of supervision of youthful members of a family. Clifford (1978:72) also recognizes that most industrialized societies no longer have strong internal and informal social controls which render crime prevention much less effective.

Recent Developments

Recent theorizing in the DM vein uses the triad of modernization, power and civilization to compose a comprehensive macro-structural explanatory framework which may be applied to explain different criminological developments in diverse societies (Heiland and Shelley, 1991:18). The added two dimensions of this framework can be viewed as strengthening the explanatory power of the DM perspective. First, the civilization concept, drawn from Elias' Civilization Theory (1982), provides the link between the long-term structural changes and the alteration of personality structures. At the individual level, Elias (1982) suggests that historically there has been an ever increasing refinement of customs and manners, an obvious pacification of the conditions of daily life and an intensification of instinctive and affected inhibitions. At the institutional level, Elias (1982) found three key societal factors to the development of greater individual control: 1) the monopolization of the instruments of power; 2) the centralization of state power; and 3) the creation of power monopoly.

According to Elias, the limitations on individual behavior can only find equilibrium when they are part of a relatively stable and easily comprehensible arrangement of actions by the broader society. And such a situation occurs when there is a monopoly of social institutions (Heiland and Shelley, 1991:3). If Elias' hypothesis holds true, that interpersonal relations vary with the civilization of society, then so should the nature of interpersonal violence and crime (Heiland and Shelley, 1991). And it would not be unreasonable to hypothesize that a more civilized society would have lower volumes of violent crimes but higher volumes of self-inflicted harmful behaviors such as drug use or suicide.

Empirical Research on the Durkheimian-Modernization Perspective

The DM perspective has been widely criticized for its simplicity and rigidity, and for its overestimation of the influence of urbanization and industrialization on crime and for its lack of consistent empirical support (Neuman and Berger, 1988; Bennett, 1991; Huggins, 1985; Sumner, 1982; Shelley, 1991). In his "Inequality, Unemployment and Crime: A Cross-National Analysis," Krohn (1976) reconfirms the research of Wolf (1971) and Wellford (1974) that the homicide rate is inversely related to the level of economic development and that property crime is positively correlated with the degree of modernization. Stack (1978) argues that Krohn's (1976) findings are to be viewed with suspicion, since they are based on noncomparable data on unemployment (e.g., Krohn uses data from 38 nations, but comparable data exist for only 8 nations).

In "A Durkheimian Analysis of International Crime Rates," Krohn (1978) evaluates the emergence of the division of labor and the consequent state of anomie as predictors of the variance in international crime. Durkheim predicts the possibility that a chronic state of anomie occurring with industrialization would produce an increased crime rate. Krohn (1978) uses homicide rate, property crime rate and total crime rate as the dependent variables from the official crime statistics of 33 developing and industrialized nations. Five independent variables include population, size, moral density, industrialization, division of labor and anomie. They are obtained from the *World Handbook of Political and Social Indicators*. The test results based on correlation and regression analysis indicate that the variable of anomie was not predictive of crime rates.

A Durkheimian model of societal development and homicide is formatted and tested by Messner (1982). Relying heavily on Giddens (1971) reinterpretation of Durkheim's *Division of Labor* (1964), it is argued that development has no overall effect on the societal homicide rate, primarily because the egalitarian changes accompanying development make for new forms of social solidarity. It is predicted that there will be no significant zero-order correlation between development and homicide, a positive partial effect of measures of moral individualism on homicide, and a negative partial effect of a measure of equality on homicide. The results from Messner's (1982) cross-sectional analysis for a sample of 50 nations provide partial support for the theory.

Hartnagal (1982) examined the relationship between modernization and female crime rates. A model is tested that incorporates female participation in various social roles as an intervening variable. Modernization is predicted to have positive, direct effects on female property crime, as well as positive, indirect effects through female role participation. Correlational and regression techniques were performed on the data from 40 countries. Little support was found for the general model. Gross national product per capita exhibits positive, direct effects on female theft and fraud. The net effects of the several female role-participation variables are generally small. In a further test of the convergence hypothesis which suggests that modernization leads toward increased female crime, and, as gender roles become more alike, female crime should increase toward the level of male crime, Hartnagal and Mizanuddin's (1986) cross-national analysis of 14 developed and 23 developing countries fails to support this theory.

Shichor (1985) uses a cross-national study to examine the effects of development on official crime rates of homicide and larceny. His findings indicate that modernization usually brings with it more reported larceny and somewhat less reported homicides. Grove et al. (1985) observe that prior research on the relationship between modernization and homicide has reported positive, null, and negative relationships. They argue that some of the ambiguity in this literature is due to the widespread use of unreliable INTERPOL homicide statistics. In general, they state, theoretical and methodological problems are a great source of ambiguity. In particular, prior research has equated modernization with increased gross domestic product (GDP) and has ignored important noneconomic aspects of modernization. The authors construct a structural equation model of modernization and homicide. Their analyses show that GDP has a weak negative direct effect on homicide. Its indirect effects, operating through several noneconomic aspects of modernization, are larger but positive, resulting in a small positive net relationship.. Religious ecology variables included in the model have uniformly weak effects on homicide, indicating that this cultural variable plays a minor role at best in the phenomenon. Two other cultural variables, school enrollments and agricultural employment, however, have substantively large effects on homicide.

Lester (1987) studied the cross-national correlations among religion, suicide and homicide among 18 industrial nations. Using religiosity variables such as religious book production, divorce rate, percent Catholic population and suicide and homicide rates, Lester's analysis indicates that the religious variables are not related to either suicide or homicide rates. This study seems to cast doubt on the Durkheimian hypothesis of the role of religion in social integration and regulation. However, the author realizes that his measures of religious behavior in this study may not have accurately measured the religiosity of the population studied.

Neuman and Berger (1988: 300) provide an overall assessment of the dominant Durkheimian-Modernization (DM) perspective in comparative criminology. After reviewing seventeen cross-national crime studies, the authors only found weak support for this perspective. They conclude that "the strength of the DM perspective lies in its emphasis on the internalized moral/normative structures which translate macro-level cultural processes into individuals' motivation to commit crime. The DM approach's neglect of political-economic and micro-ecological factors, and its lack of support in empirical studies, limit its ability to serve as the general framework for future research."

Rogers (1989) notes that theories of crime have long assumed that increased criminality is an inevitable consequence of economic and social progress. This view, which was accepted by scholars who built on Durkheimian modernization theory, was left unchallenged by the dependency theorists of the 1970s. However, historical studies of crime have now undermined this assumption by showing that in many nations industrialization, urbanization, and rapid social change have been accompanied by declines in crime. Rogers (1989) recommends that more studies of long-term trends of crime and criminal law are needed before a necessarily complex theory of crime can be advanced.

Bennett (1991) provides a pooled cross-sectional time-series analysis for two competing theoretical models: the Durkheimian model vs. the opportunity model. The Durkheimian model's predicted relationship between economic development and crime is refuted. The opportunity model only received partial support. However, Bennett's (1991) research reveals interesting nonlinear effects that allow further specification of the crime and development relationship.

Leavitt (1992) tests Durkheim's (1938) hypothesis relating increasing crime frequency to social differentiation as a process of socio-cultural evolution. A cross-cultural sample of 121 societies representing a broad range of societal development, geographical dispersion, and cultural diversity was selected. While it is recognized that crime is not defined the same across all societal types, fourteen measures ranging across the following seven behavioral categories are analyzed: (1) violent acts against persons (homicide, assault, rape and sexual attack, and robbery); (2) property crimes (larceny, burglary, and vandalism); (3) vice (gambling, prostitution, and drug use); (4) fraud; (5) juvenile delinquency; (6) professional crime (career crime); and (7) organized crime. The measures of social differentiation include the division of labor, social inequality in socioeconomic and political forms, community size and density. Leavitt's (1992) empirical analysis supports Durkheim's hypothesis that increasing crime frequency is related to the process of social differentiation.

Ortega et al. (1992) point out that previous cross-national research testing the Durkheimian-Modernization hypothesis is flawed because of two reasons: (1) it assessed the criminogenic consequences of different levels of economic development rather than changes in development; and (2) it failed to control for the confounding effects of changes in the age structure of populations. Using pooled cross-sectional and time-series INTERPOL data from 1969 to 1982 for 51 countries, Ortega et al.'s (1992) study supported the Durkheimian-Modernization hypothesis for both homicide and theft rates.

Unnithan and Whitt (1992) tested a theoretical tradition (the "stream analogy") predating Emile Durkheim which links suicide and homicide as two currents in a single stream, lethal violence. Using data from a sample of 31 nations on homicide and suicide rates from 1950 to 1970, the authors examined inequality and economic development as two determinants of the total lethal violence rate (suicide + homicide), the suicide proportion of total lethal violence and separate homicide and suicide rates. Inequality was found to be curvilinearly related to homicide and total lethal violence, and negatively related to suicide and the proportion of suicide in total lethal violence. Economic development was unrelated to the total lethal violence rate, weakly related to suicide and homicide, and curvilinearly related to the proportion of suicide in total lethal violence.

Huang (1995) argues that previous cross-national tests of the Durkheimian-Modernization theory on murder assume urbanization, industrialization, maternal absence and population density are positively correlated with national murder rate. They do not explain, however, which forces restrain most people from killing each other. Based on Durkheim's writing, Huang (1995) proposes that moral individualism, characterized by respect for personal dignity and individual rights, is a barrier to committing murder. His multivariate pooled cross-sectional time-series analysis of 29 countries (1975-1980) based on United Nations' Crime Survey data supports this Durkheimian hypothesis.

Summary and Conclusion

As one of the most dominant comparative criminological theories, the Durkheimian Modernization perspective has been frequently discussed, tested and revised. However, controversies have been generated during the process of operationalizing concepts of the Durkheimian-Modernization perspective; for example, the level of economic development vs. rate of growth. Empirical research is also inconclusive. There are calls for further theoretical development which will incorporate those often neglected aspects, such as moral individualism and penal evolution that are found in Durkheim's writings on crime. Researchers also demand further methodological sophistication such as using pooled cross-sectional time series analysis with a common set of control variables and testing non-linear relationships.

Chapter IV

Theory Modification and Elaboration: Theoretical Frameworks for Current Study

Elaborated Durkheimian Modernization Theory

General Theoretical Framework

It is evident that the Durkheimian Modernization perspective on crime has been the dominating force in the field of comparative criminology. However, empirical tests in the past attest to the necessity for further theoretical refinement and methodological improvement. Heiland and Shelley (1991:18) argue that the "triad of modernization, power and civilization" can be applied to construct a comprehensive macro-structural explanatory framework which may be able to explain different criminological developments in diverse societies. Figure 1 illustrates a framework which consolidates the original Durkheimian propositions and aspects from the more recent Heiland and Shelley's (1991) proposition on crime.

Figure 1
Durkheimian Perspective on Crime

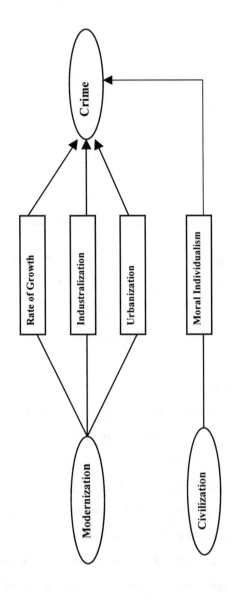

Theory Decomposition

One of the major causal relationships indicated by this framework lies between the concept of modernization and crime. Modernization is measured by the following three concepts: urbanization, industrialization and rate of growth. Urbanization was frequently used in previous empirical studies (e.g., Bennett, 1991; Gurr et al., 1977; Hansmann and Quigley, 1982; Kick and LaFree, 1985; Krahn et al., 1986; Krohn, 1978; Krohn and Wellford, 1977; LaFree and Kick, 1986; Lodhi and Tilly, 1973; McDonald, 1976; Messner, 1982; Quinney, 1965; Wolf, 1971; Zehr, 1976). In the Durkheimian Modernization model, urbanization is an indicator of moral density that leads to increases in the division of labor and crime (Bennett, 1991:345). Although it can be hypothesized that urbanization and crime rates increase together, empirical findings which are mostly based on cross-sectional design are inconsistent. Shelley (1981:139) suggests that:

> *cities during the initial phase of urbanization experience increased rates of violence simultaneously with new levels of property crime. Only as urbanization progresses, as migration into urban centers subsides, and as the newly arrived urban inhabitants adjust to city life, does the total crime rate decline. Crimes of violence cede their once preeminent place to offenses against property.*

In the current study, I will use a pooled cross-sectional time series design to examine the impact of urbanization on crime in two different sub-samples: developed countries and developing countries.

Industrialization is the other indicator often applied in the Durkheimian Modernization perspective on crime (e.g., Avison and Loring, 1986; Bennett and Basiotis, 1991; Hansmann and Quigley, 1982; Braithwaite and Braithwaite, 1980; Conklin and Simpson, 1985; Groves et al., 1985; Hartnagel, 1982; Krahn et al., 1986; Kick and LaFree, 1985; Krohn, 1976, 1978; Krohn and Wellford, 1977; Messner, 1980, 1982, 1985; Wellford, 1974). Finally, the rate of economic growth has been proposed by Ortega et al. (1992) as a third way of measuring the degree of modernization of society.

The second causal link exists between civilization and crime. Since the Durkheimian Modernization theory was criticized for overestimating the influence of urbanization and industrialization on crime (Bennett, 1991; Huggins, 1985; Sumner, 1982), new theorizing in the Durkheimian Modernization vein emphasizes the process of civilization and its effect on crime in an effort to explain the long term decline in interpersonal violence (Barberet, 1994; Gurr, 1989; Heiland and Shelley, 1991; van Dijk, 1989). Drawing from the writings of Durkheim (1958) and Elias (1982), Barberet (1994:13) argues that in civilized societies where normative regulation has adapted to the changes in the division of labor, moral individualism should prevent people from killing or stealing from each other.

Apparently, the concept of civilization has yet to be incorporated into a testable Durkheimian theoretical framework. It has been argued that modernization and civilization do not necessarily correspond with each other (Heiland and Shelley, 1991:17). It is more arguable that both the definition and the operationalization of this concept invite enigmatic challenge. To operationalize the concept of civilization, van Dijk (1989:201) suggests that the nature of a society's policy on crime reflects its level of civilization. He proposes that the types and levels of sanctions imposed by a society can be used as a measure of civilization. Heiland and Shelley (1991:3) observe that the development process of civilization in the western context is accompanied by decriminalization of penal law, greater tolerance of deviant behavior, reduction of lengthy imprisonment, fewer sanctions and the creation of prison alternatives. I believe, however, that fitting the puzzle of the civilization concept into the elaborated Durkheim Modernization framework requires further theoretical exercise.

In *Civilization in General and Types of Civilization*, Durkheim (1902) asks how a society, which is only a composite of relatively independent parts and differentiated organs, can nevertheless form an individuality endowed with an unity which is analogous to that of individual personalities. He suggests that:

Very possibly one of the factors which most contributes to this result is that poorly analyzed complex which is termed the civilization appropriate to each social type and even, more especially, to each society. This is because there is in every civilization a kind of tonality sui generis which is to be found in all the details of collective life.

The character of people is another factor of the same kind. In a society, as in an individual, the character is the central and permanent nucleus which joins together the various moments of an existence and which gives succession and continuity to life.

Moreover, it can be divined that the question of types of civilization and that of types of collective characters must be closely linked (Durkheim, 1902:167-68).

Indeed, "that poorly analyzed complex which is termed the civilization" needs to be conceptualized and operationalized. I argue that Durkheim's standpoint on moral individualism can be synthesized to approximate his concept of civilization.

In this study, I use moral individualism as a measure of civilization representing the collective character of a society. My justification, based on Durkheim, is that a society is more civilized if it evolves toward greater individuation; i.e., it cultivates greater moral individualism, which encompasses among other things such values as compassion, rationalism, freedom, social justice, and democracy. I assume that a measure of moral individualism yields an estimate of the level of civilization for a particular society.

Dynamic Marxian Economic Theory on Crime

Prelude to the New Theoretical Framework

Consistent with Marx's assumptions about human nature--i.e., that an individual's actions depend on his social relationships and his social relationships depend on his class situation and economic structure of his society, those who have less stake in wealth, status and power are more likely to be demoralized and are more easily subject to crime or vice. Taylor et al. (1973, 1975) suggest crime be studied as one significant consequence of exploitation and oppression of the working class under capitalism. They also argue that models of crime causation in the Marxist tradition must include a macro-level analysis which incorporates a political economy of crime (Taylor et al., 1973). Quinney (1980), on the other hand, proposes to understand crime as an inevitable response to the material conditions of capitalism. He sees predatory crimes such as burglary and robbery as reproducing a capitalist system of acquisition of property by expropriating the income and property of others. Moreover, Quinney sees violent crimes such as murder, assault and rape as crimes of accommodation committed by those who were brutalized by the capitalist system.

Lynch and Grove (1986:45-46) summarize three major criticisms of the radical Marxist criminological approach: (1) Marxist criminologists view crime simply as the mirror image of control and they see the only cause of crime to be law; (2) Marxist criminologists have limited themselves to an oversimplified unicausal approach where the only source of crime is capitalism; and (3) Marxist criminologists neglect empirical research. Responding to these criticisms, Lynch and Grove (1986:46) propose that capitalism has at its core a conflict between capital and labor. Lynch et al. (1994) call for a reorientation of radical criminology by making Marx's economic theory of surplus value as the cornerstone of theory construction. They claim that such a reorientation can create an empirically testable explanation of crime consistent with Marx's world view. They further suggest that the relationship between surplus value and crime be tested in other countries besides the United States.

Much of the existing research and theorizing on cross-national application of Marxian perspective on crime has focused on the so called "Marxian World-System Theory," i.e., the study of the impact of the global economy and uneven expansion of the capitalist mode of production on crime (Chase-Dunn, 1975; Chase-Dunn and Rubinson, 1979; Humphries and Wallace, 1980; Lynch et al., 1988; Wallerstein, 1974; Walton, 1982). In a recent overview of cross-national applications of criminological theories, Neuman and Berger (1988) criticize that the Marxian-World

System perspective is too limited and that it can not explain criminal behaviors at individual level.

General Theoretical Framework

Responding to Lynch et al.'s (1994) call for testing Marxian economic theory examining surplus value and crime in cross-national context, I develop a dynamic Marxian economic perspective on crime. Figure 2 illustrates the major theoretical linkages involved in this perspective.

Marx views capital as the primary productive entity in capitalist society; and capital is seen as producing a surplus value. Therefore, surplus value is used as an indicator for capital condition in this framework. Barlow and Johnson (1996) have used economic indicators such as the annual percent change in GNP, corporate profits, the excess of export over import merchandise for a given year, business failure rate and the number of banks closed as measures of capital condition. For theoretical purpose in this research, it seems justifiable to include surplus value as the indicator to tap this important dimension in a dynamic Marxian economic theory on crime.

A nation's location in the world system is used to capture the international dimension of the Marxian economic theory on crime. Unemployment is used to reflect labor condition. Government expenditure on social welfare, education and health are employed to reflect human investment. Together, these four dimensions: condition of capital, condition of labor, world system and human investment, constitute a dynamic Marxian economic theory on crime.

Theory Decomposition

According to Marx (1974), capital accumulation - one of his basic economic concepts - depends on the extraction of surplus value from the labor force. Lynch et al. (1994:18) argue that Marx sees the rate of surplus value as an objective measure of labor's alienation or exploitation by capital. The theory of surplus value is also

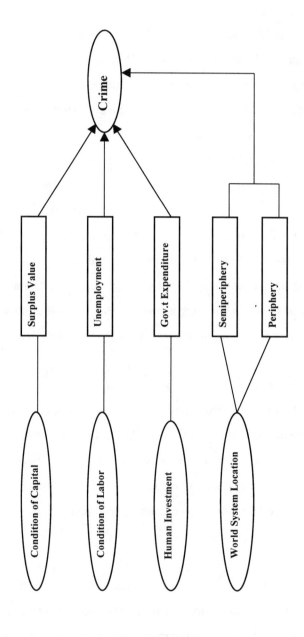

Figure 2
Marxian Perspective on Crime

regarded as capable of defining a complex model of crime which ties together social structure and individual opportunities, motivations and choices (Groves and Frank, 1987; Lynch and Groves, 1989; Lynch et al., 1994). In particular, such an explanation suggests that "the extraction of surplus value increases the disparity of wealth between classes, causes the concentration of capital in the hands of a few, generates economically and socially marginal populations, and structures choices and opportunity" (Lynch et al., 1994:22). Accordingly, those who hold this perspective would hypothesize that the higher the rate of surplus value, the greater the number of people who are made socially and economically marginal to the means of production and, thus, the higher the crime rate.

The location of a nation in the world system not only determines its international economic and political relations with other countries, it also affects the structural context of its own development including class relations and domestic policies (Lynch et al., 1988). Humphries and Wallace (1980) argue that urban crime is the result of uneven expansion and contraction of the capitalist production process within and between nations. Timberlake and Kentor (1983) also suggest that overurbanization in periphery nations is criminogenic. Lynch et al. (1988:7) concur that urbanization and industrialization are outcomes of attempts to expand capitalism, and crime increases with such an expansion of capitalism. Lynch et al. (1988), however, construct different hypotheses according to the location of a country in the world system. They hypothesize that (1) core nations will have higher rates of property crime, due to democratic and egalitarian ideologies and relative deprivation; and (2) periphery nations will have higher rates of violent crime, due to political repression, frustration-aggression reactions and alienation.

The inclusion of unemployment in a dynamic Marxian economic theory on crime is consistent with Marx's argument about the lumpenproletariat--those who are unemployed, underemployed, unproductive and demoralized. Marx argues that the lumpenproletariat is subject to all forms of crime and vice (Hirst, 1972). According to Marx (1982:20), "it is not the consciousness of men that determines their existence, but, on the contrary, their social existence determines their consciousness". If this logic holds, criminal activities can be seen as such an expression of the individual consciousness reflecting his social existence; e.g., be unemployed.

Structuralist Marxists argue that the state is itself fragmented and composed of various competing agencies, each with their own interests (Spitzer, 1980; Jessop, 1982). In fact, evidence suggests that governmental efforts of providing guarantees of minimal levels of material well-being are associated with comparatively lower levels of serious crime (Messner and Rosenfeld, 1997:102). The variable-government expenditures on human services-which consolidates: 1) government expenditures on social welfare; 2) government expenditures on health; and 3) government expenditures on education, is included in the framework. This new variable reflects the concept of government human investment. It demonstrates the governmental position with respect to reducing public anxiety, especially among the poor, to counterbalance the capitalist market force. In accordance with the Marxian assumption that one's social existence determines his individual consciousness, the more benefits (e.g., social welfare, health care and education) a government can provide, the less dependent on the capitalist market outcomes its citizens become. The less dependent their livelihood on the market fluctuation, the less demoralized and alienated the public would be. The less the demoralization and alienation, the less the desire for committing crimes of accommodation.

Given the previous research findings, I think that it is theoretically relevant to explore the possible interaction effects between development factors such as urbanization, industrialization, economic growth and the world system status. The world system dimension of the dynamic Marxian perspective on crime suggest that urbanization, industrialization as well as economic growth could have distinctive criminogenic impacts on nations with different world system status. In this study, I use the detailed classification of world-system location developed by Snyder and Kick (1979) (see Appendix I for more details). For exploratory purposes, I construct and test a synthesized model (see Figure 3) which incorporates variables from both

Figure 3
A Synthesized Developmental Model

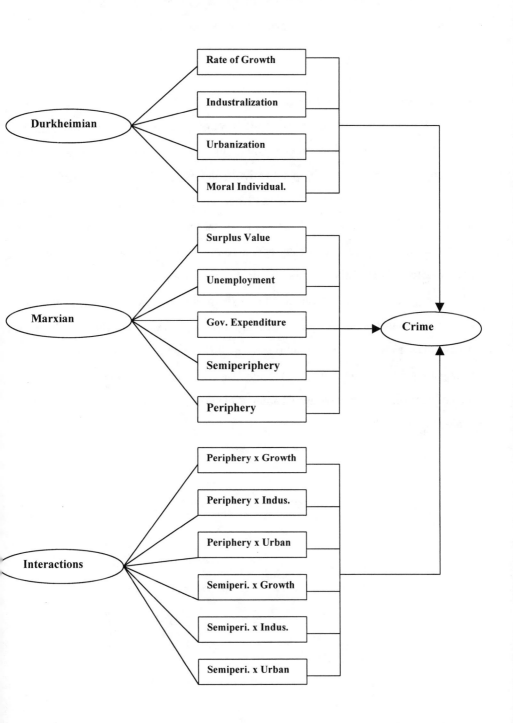

the Durkheimian and the Marxian perspectives with variables reflecting the interactive effects between the developmental factors and different world system status.

Chapter Summary and Conclusion

The elaborated Durkheimian Modernization perspective has two dimensions: modernization (urbanization, rate of growth, industrialization) and civilization. The dynamic Marxian Economic perspective consists of four dimensions: capital condition, position in world system, labor condition, and government human investment. The major task of this study is to test the Durkheimian and the Marxian perspectives proposed in this chapter. A common set of control variables will be used in each of the statistical models constructed based on these two perspectives. Moreover, a test will also be conducted of a synthesized developmental model which incorporates all the variables included in both the Marxian and the Durkheimian perspectives, as well as the interactions terms. Although not the focus of this study, testing a synthesized developmental model can contribute to future theorizing in the field of comparative criminology. Chapter V discusses the blueprint for the empirical analysis.

Chapter V

Methodological Issues in Quantitative Comparative Criminological Research

Data Sources

Description of Data Sets

Empirical data used for this research are largely drawn from the following sources: Comparative Crime Data File (CCDF) by Archer and Gartner (1984), the Second (1975-1980) and Third (1980-1986) U.N. Surveys of Crime Trends, Operations of Criminal Justice Systems and Crime Prevention Strategies by the United Nations (1991) and Correlates of Crime (COC) data archive developed by Richard Bennett (1989). Among the three, CCDF and U.N.'s crime data serve as the major sources for my crime data and the others supply the necessary information needed for the construction of the explanatory variables for the analysis. In addition to data already available on disks, I collected other variable information from the *Yearbook of National Accounts Statistics* and the *United Nations' Demographic Yearbook* for various years.

The CCDF data cover the crime rates of 110 societies and 44 major cities from 1900 to the early 1970s. Crimes include murder, manslaughter, homicide, rape, assault, robbery, and theft. The United Nation's crime surveys (WCS, 2nd and 3rd surveys) provide crime, criminal and criminal justice data for the time period of 1975 to 1985. The following crime and criminal information are available: crimes recorded by police, offenses committed, intentional homicide, non-intentional homicide, assault, drug crimes, rape, kidnapping, robbery, theft, fraud and embezzlement, bribery and corruption, person apprehended, person prosecuted, person convicted. The third data set, the Correlates of Crime (COC) data archive contains quantitative data on crime, social, political and economic indicators covering the 25-year period from 1960 to 1984 for 52 nations in which 49 nations are included in my sample.

Merging The Data Sets

To facilitate my statistical analyses, two sets of data files were constructed and saved separately (1) a cross-sectional data set in which the nation is the unit of analysis (N = 49); and (2) a pooled data set in which nation-year is the unit of analysis (N=1250).

1) Cross-Sectional Data Set

Merging the data sets already on disks involved the following steps: (1) limit all the three data sets, i.e., CCDF, WCS and COC to cover only the time period from 1960 to 1984; (2) apply the "country code" used in Bennett's (1992) COC data and transform all other country codings into an identical coding; (3) merge the three data sets into a cross-sectional master data file using this uniform "country code" as the criterion. Additional collection of variable information from other sources were added to this cross-sectional master file.

2) Pooled Data Set

After the cross-sectional data set was completed, I transformed it into a pooled cross-sectional time-series data format. In the pooled data file all observations of a particular cross-sectional unit are together. This data format requires a complete time-series for the first group (nation, in my case) followed by a time-series for the second group; e.g., Australia from 1960 to 1984, followed by a time-series for the second group and Canada from 1960 to 1984. With N cross-sectional units observed for T time periods the total number of observations will be N x T in the data set.

Samples

As in many quantitative cross-national studies, my sample size is limited by the availability of data. To maximize the use of available data for both dependent and explanatory variables, I include homicide and theft data covering a 25-year period from 1960 to 1984 for a diverse sample of 49 nations. Although not randomly selected, my sample includes both developed and developing nations and nations from every region of the world. They represent a wide range of types of economy, political environments and legal systems. Socialist countries, due to lack of data, are not included.

To ameliorate the problems of sampling bias and generalizability, I categorize nations in my general sample into two sub-samples, i.e., a sample of developed countries and a sample of developing countries. Descriptive statistics of different samples are compared and discussed later. Table 1 provides the list of nations included in my sample.

Operationalization of Variables

Measurement of the Dependent Variables

In this study, two major categories of crime from the Comparative Crime Data File (CCDF) and the UN's World Crime Survey (WCS) offense data serve as dependent variables: (1) homicide, which refers to death purposely or non purposely inflicted by another person, including murder, homicide, infanticide, manslaughter but excluding traffic accidents resulting in death; and (2) theft which refers to the stealthy taking away of property without the owners' consent, including both simple

Table 1:   Sample Members

Total Sample of Nations (N = 49):

Developed Nations (n = 20):

Australia	Austria	Canada	Denmark	England/Wales
Finland	France	Germany	Greece	Italy
Japan	Luxembourg	Netherlands	New Zealand	Norway
Portugal	Scotland	Spain	Sweden	United States

Developing Nations (n = 29):

Brunei	Burma	Chile	Cyprus	Egypt
Fiji	Hong Kong	India	Indonesia	Israel
Ivory Coast	Jamaica	Kenya	Korea	Kuwait
Lebanon	Libya	Malawi	Malaysia	Morocco
Monaco	Nigeria	Peru	Philippines	Singapore
Sri Lanka	Syria	Turkey	Zambia	

---

* Categorization of the developed and developing nations are based on the definitions provided in the United Nations' Demographic Yearbook.

and aggravated theft as defined by criminal law of each country, theft of a motor vehicle, burglary and house breaking. Rates per 100,000 are constructed for each variable by dividing the total number of offenses by that year's national population.

Measurement of the Independent Variables

   1) For the Dynamic Marxian Economic Perspective

   Rate of surplus value (SURPLUS) is calculated by using a formula originated from the following equation:

$$\text{surplus value} = \text{surplus product} / \text{variable capital}$$

$$= [\,(\text{value added} - \text{workers' wage}) / \text{workers' wage}\,] * 100$$

Several researchers have employed the above formula to calculate Marx's rate of surplus value (Amsden, 1981; Cueno, 1978, 1982, 1984; Lynch, 1988; Lynch et al., 1994) among productive laborers in manufacturing sectors. In the current study, I make some adjustment to this equation. First, I decided to use value added for all economic activities rather than for a particular kind of economic activity such as manufacturing. Second, compensation of employees rather than the workers' wage is used. Compensation of employees includes: (1) all wages and salaries, in cash and in kind, paid to employees; (2) employers' contributions to social security plans and to private employee welfare plans for the account of their employees; and (3) employers' contributions to private pension funds, family allowances, health and other casualty insurance, life insurance and similar plans for the account of their employees (United Nations, 1986). There are two reasons for making these adjustments: (1) I am more interested in studying the criminogenic impact of the rate of surplus value in a dynamic capitalist economy than in focusing on a single sector of the economy such as manufacturing; (2) I argue that using compensation of employees is more appropriate than using workers' wage in the rate of surplus value formula. Given the tremendous historical, economic and political changes since Marx's time, workers' wage alone can no longer adequately capture the concept of variable capital cost, i.e., the value of labor, which appears to be much more complicated in modern capitalist states.

I create two dummy variables to capture a nation's world-system status. The first is coded 1 for periphery nations (PERIPH), and 0 otherwise. The second is coded 1 for semi-periphery nations (SEMIPERI), and 0 otherwise. Core nations are the omitted category.

Unemployment (UNEMP) is measured as the percentage of unemployed in the total civilian labor force. Government expenditure (GOVEXP) is measured as the total percentage of the government expenditures in social security, social welfare, health and education.

2) For the Durkheimian-Modernization Perspective

Rate of economic growth (GROWTH_1) is measured as the difference between the GDP per capita in two consecutive years. Urbanization (URBAN) is measured as the yearly percentage of a nation's population residing in urban areas. Industrialization (INDUS) is measured as the ratio of a nation's GDP in the manufacturing sector to the nation's GDP.

Moral individualism is measured by the sum of scores of political rights and civil rights which represents the concern for individual rights and personal dignity in a society (see Appendix II for more details). Scores are reverse-coded so that higher values indicate greater civil and political rights. Data for these scores were collected by Gastil (1986) in Comparative Survey of Freedom.[1]

3) For the Synthesized Developmental Model

The interaction terms of Urbanization x Periphery or Urbanization x Semi-periphery are measured as the products of the yearly percentage of a nation's population residing in urban areas and the Periphery or Semi-periphery nation status dummy variables. The interaction terms of Industrialization x Periphery or Industrialization x Semi-periphery are measured as the products of the ratio of a nation's GDP in the manufacturing sector to the nation's GDP and the Periphery or Semi-periphery nation status dummy variables. The interaction terms of Economic growth x Periphery or Economic growth x Semi-periphery are measured as the differences between the GDP per capita in two consecutive years and the Periphery or Semi-periphery nation status dummy variables.

Measurement of Control Variables

Divorce rate is measured as the number of divorces per thousand population. Female labor force participation is measured as the proportion of the female population that participates in the labor force. Population change (POP_1) is measured as the difference between the population of a nation in two consecutive years.

Hypotheses

Based on the theoretical framework introduced in Chapter IV, I specify the following hypotheses for each of the two perspectives: the elaborated Durkheim-Modernization perspective (DM) and the dynamic Marxian Economic perspective (ME). I also construct hypotheses for the interaction terms included in a synthesized developmental model in which variables from both the Durkheimian and the Marxian perspectives are present.

Elaborated Durkheimian Modernization Perspective (DM)

   1) Modernization and Crime

      Hypothesis DM1:

> *The rate of economic development, rather than the level of economic development, is indicative of the disruption of the traditional support mechanisms in societies undergoing rapid social changes. Crime occurs when there are no longer strong internal and informal social controls which can render effective crime prevention. There is a positive relationship between the rate of economic growth and crime.*

Hypothesis DM2:

> *Industrialization changes a society from the one characterized by mechanical solidarity with little division of labor to one characterized by organic solidarity with a complex division of labor. Crime occurs when the normative systems fail to keep up with the change in the division of labor. I predict a positive relationship between industrialization and crime.*

Hypothesis DM3:

> *Urbanization increases moral density which leads to increased division of labor. I predict a positive relationship between urbanization and crime.*

2) Civilization and Crime

Hypothesis DM4:

> *A nation with greater moral individualism is more civilized and will have lower crime rates.*

Dynamic Marxian-Economic Perspective (ME)

1) Capital Condition and Crime

Hypothesis ME1:

> *Higher surplus value gained by the capitalists will induce greater alienation and demoralization on workers. Both homicide and theft, as crimes of accommodation, will be likely to occur more often when the surplus value gained is high.*

2) World System and Crime

Hypothesis ME2:

> *Periphery and Semi-periphery nations will have higher rates of violent crime compared to Core nations, due to political*

repression, frustration-aggression reactions and alienation (cf. Lynch et al., 1988).

Hypothesis ME3:

Core nations will have higher rates of theft compared to Periphery and Semi-periphery nations, due to democratic and egalitarian ideologies and relative deprivation (cf. Lynch et al., 1988).

3) Labor Condition and Crime

Hypothesis ME4:

Unemployment deteriorates the labor condition, heightens the economic stress and increases demoralization. I predict a positive relationship between unemployment and crime.

4) Human Investment and Crime

Hypothesis ME5:

The more the government spends on social welfare, health and education (human investment), the less citizens depend on the capitalist market outcomes for assuring their wealth, health and their potentials of successfully participating the capitalist market, making them less demoralized and alienated. I predict a negative relationship between the amount of government human investment and crime.

A Synthesized Developmental Model (SD)

Hypothesis SD1:

The relationship between development and crime depends on a nation's world system location. There will be less criminogenic impact of development on crimes in Core nations than in Periphery and Semi-periphery nations.

Hypothesis SD2:

> *The relationship between urbanization and crime depends on a nation's world system location. There will be less criminogenic impact of urbanization on crimes in Core nations than in Periphery and Semi-periphery nations.*

Hypothesis SD3:

> *The relationship between industrialization and crime depends on a nation's world system location. There will be less criminogenic impact of industrialization on crimes in Core nations than in Periphery and Semi-periphery nations.*

Data Quality Issues

The Problem of Erratic Data Reporting For the Dependent Variable

The erratic reporting of crime data has been one of the major research obstacles for those who are interested in cross-national criminological studies. When confronted with problems of having crime data that are only available for certain years but not for others, most researchers use the averages for multiyear periods in order to boost the sample size as well as to enhance the reliability of the estimate (e.g., Archer & Gartner, 1984; Avison & Loring, 1986; Braithwaite & Braithwaite, 1989; Kick & LaFree, 1986; Krahn et al., 1986; McDonald, 1976; Messner, 1989, 1992). The very logic of averaging, as pointed out by Messner (1992) in his analysis of the impact of erratic data reporting for homicide, is to redress the possible measurement errors which might have been induced by the factor of the instability of homicide reporting.

Using INTERPOL, WHO and CCDF crime data, Messner (1992) simulated a test by first selecting a sample of nations with complete homicide data for a specified time interval and computing the average homicide rate based on all years in this interval (i.e., the baseline rate). Next, he produced alternative estimates of average homicide rates based on different and smaller number of years . All these alternatives estimates were then correlated with the baseline rate. As a result, Messner (1992:167) argues that "for samples of nations that report homicide data with a reasonable degree of regularity, the use of information for a subset of years rather than the entire period of interest is unlikely to alter the results of the research". However, Messner (1992:168) warns that the situation for nations with lower reporting frequencies is more problematic because "this instability could be a product of high levels of genuine fluctuations in homicide activity, or it could be a product of high levels of measurement error. He further suggests that some type of weighting procedure be employed to assign different weights to cases (countries) that involve homicide estimates based on incomplete data and exhibit different levels of reporting (Messner, 1992:169).

Weighted Least Square (WLS): A Remedial Measure

Responding to Messner's (1992) call for improvement of the treatment of erratic data for countries with varying degrees of levels of reporting, I will examine my data and explore the utility of Weighted Least Square (WLS) in this situation. One method applying Weighted Least Square (WLS) is a five-stage process based on Studenmund's (1992) suggestions.

First, I need to test whether there is heteroskedasticity in the error terms. For example, I want to know that in equation 1, whether the variance of the error terms-VAR(ϵ_i) is a constant σ^2, or a function of some other variable Z, i.e., $\sigma^2 Z_i^2$. In both equation 1 and 2, i indicates that the variance can change from observation to observation.

$$Y_i = \beta_0 + \beta_1 X_{1i} + \beta_2 X_{2i} + \epsilon_i \qquad [1]$$

$$Y_i = \beta_0 + \beta_1 X_{1i} + \beta_2 X_{2i} + Z_i u_i \qquad [2]$$

In any event, previous research findings can be used to help identify a variable (i.e., Z) which is suspected to be related to the error variance.

Second, a base line regression is run based on equation 1, and the residual (ϵ) of this regression analysis is saved. Third, Park's test of heteroskedasticity in the error terms is applied which uses a function of the residuals as the dependent variable of a second regression whose explanatory variable is a function of the suspected proportionality factor Z.

$$\ln(\epsilon_i^2) = \beta_0 + \beta_1 \ln Z_i + u_i \qquad [3]$$

Fourth, I run the equation 3 model and see whether the unstandardized regression coefficient for the suspected proportionality factor Z (β_1) is significantly different from zero (at .05 level). If it is significant, then I reject the null hypothesis of homoskedasticity and pursue WLS procedure. Lastly, weighted least square is run to get rid of heteroskedasticity by dividing it (Z) by a function of the proportionality factor Z (Studenmund, 1992).

$$Y_i/Z_i = \beta_0/Z_i + \beta_1 X_{1i}/Z_i + \beta_2 X_{2i}/Z_i + Z_i u_i/Z_i \qquad [4]$$

Equation 4 can also be simplified as:

$$Y_i/Z_i = \beta_0/Z_i + \beta_1 X_{1i}/Z_i + \beta_2 X_{2i}/Z_i + u_i \qquad [5]$$

The equation 5 satisfies the classical regression assumption--no heteroskedastic error terms.

The Problem of Sample Selection Bias

Sampling has always been one of the most critical aspects in sociological research methods. Sample selection bias exists whenever potential observations from some population of interest are excluded from a sample on a nonrandom basis. In the current study, I also risk sample selection bias as a result of incidental selection of my sample. In my cross-sectional data file, I included 49 nations among which 20 are developed nations and 29 are developing nations. Although it appears that the sample nations included are roughly representing all the major regions of the world, it nevertheless is possible that they are incidentally selected according to the availability of data. In this case, I used the availability of crime data as the principal criterion in the selection process. Thus, it is possible that nations with relatively better established crime recording system are more likely to be included in my sample. One of the consequences of this would be that, when running regression analysis, the parameter estimates based on such a sample might very well be biased. The incidental sample selection procedure may also invite the danger of specification error for the model proposed.

Berk (1983:227) argues that one should not simply dismiss the problem of sample selection bias by claiming interest only in the nonrandom subset of cases represented by the sample at hand. He further suggests that in multivariate models, it is difficult to find out whether the biased regression estimates overstate or understate the true causal effects (Berk, 1983:229). Berk recommends that "perhaps the best advice is always to begin with the assumption that sample selection bias exists and proceed where possible with the corrections unless a strong argument can be made that moots the problem" (1983:235). Practically, Berk's (1983) method of correction for the sample selection bias involves a multi-stage process. First, create a dummy endogenous variable which takes the value of 1 if the observation of the dependent variable is missing and 0 when its observation is present. Second, run either probit, linear probability or logit models using this newly created dummy variable as the dependent variable and include the original set of independent variables in the model.

Third, the predicted values from this equation are saved and used to construct a hazard rate instrumental variable. Fourth, the correction factor--the hazard rate--is then treated as a new variable and included in any substantive equations. Lastly, substantive analyses are run using OLS procedure. In simple terms, Berk (1983:233) suggests that "the hazard rate from the linear probability model is equal to the predicted probability of nonresponse minus 1.0. The hazard rate from the logit model is the predicted probability of nonresponse".

The Problem of Missing Values Concerning Independent Variables

Researchers have long been arguing the proper strategies for treatment of missing values associated with the explanatory variables (Cohen & Cohen, 1975; Donner, 1982; Glasser, 1964; Wilks, 1932). For years researchers have adopted a relatively easy treatment of substituting the mean for the missing values. This procedure is fairly common and has become standard in varieties of statistical analysis packages.

Assuming there are two explanatory variables X_1 and X_2 with missing values on the latter only, Donner (1982:379) examines the relative effectiveness of four procedures commonly used for handling missing data in regression analysis: 1) the complete-case method, in which the usual least squares analysis is applied to the n cases for which both X_1 and X_2 are present; 2) the mean substitution method, in which a missing value is replaced by the mean of X_2 over the complete cases; 3) the method of linear prediction, in which a missing value is replaced by its predicted value from the simple linear regression of X_2 on X_1 over the complete cases; and 4) the piecewise method, in which the usual analysis is applied to a sample covariance matrix in which elements involving X_2 are computed from the subset of complete cases, while elements involving Y or X_1 are computed from all available observations.

Overall, Donner (1982) suggests that the mean substitution procedure is relatively effective for estimating the coefficients of incompletely observed variables when the correlations involving these variables are weak and the proportion of missing cases is fairly high. Nevertheless, he argues that the coefficient estimations resulting from this procedure tend to be biased if the correlations among the explanatory variables are strong. Such a bias will persist even in larger samples with random patterns of missing data (Donner, 1982:380).

Cohen and Cohen's (1975:285-86) dummy coding plus plugged mean method of missing data treatment "segregates the missing data effect from those of known groups, leaving their regression coefficients a function only of present data, while capitalizing on the total n for statistical power in significance tests". In Cohen and Cohen's strategy, the missing observations are substituted by means and an additional dichotomously coded dummy variable is added to the regression analysis to represent the presence or absence of missing data. Cohen and Cohen (1975:286-87) do raise a few cautions that there are circumstances where it is optimal not to use the dummy coding variable. One of the major concerns is that when it is known, or can be safely assumed, that absence of data on a research factor is random, then the inclusion of the dummy coding variable simply weakens the statistical stability and power. Another concern applies to the situation in which many independent variables with nonrandomly missing data are involved. In their own words, Cohen and Cohen (1975:286) wrote: "it would be dubious practice to have each accompanied by its own missing data code, since the resulting set of missing data variables are likely to be substantially (if not perfectly) correlated".

The Problem of Influential Cases in Data Analysis

In addition to the preceding discussions on issues of missing data in both the dependent and the independent variables, there is yet an issue concerning the problematic impact of the influential cases. Discussions on the importance of influential cases in regression analysis have demonstrated that parameter estimates can be very sensitive to a few influential cases (Gunst and Mason, 1980; Weisberg, 1980; Weede, 1986; Muller, 1986). Prior research indicates that examining residuals in regression analysis can be helpful to identify anomalies in the data which yield either poor prediction or poor parameter estimation. Gunst and Mason (1980:220-261) provide an extensive coverage on residual analysis. They suggest that studentized residuals, studentized deleted residuals combined with the distance measure-Cook's D, offer excellent diagnostic ability. Meanwhile, graphic techniques can serve as valuable compliments to these numerical rules.

Cook's D measures the distance between the estimated regression coefficients vector from the full model with all observations, and the corresponding estimated coefficients vector from the model with the ith observation removed. This statistic indicates the extent to which the prediction equation would change if the ith observation was deleted (Gunst and Mason, 1980:255). The criterion for determining a highly influential case is a value of 1.0 or greater on the Cook's D statistic (see Weisberg, 1980). It has been argued, however, that Cook's D is not a test statistic for outliers but only an indication of the closeness of the estimated regression coefficients from all observations and from any given observation deleted. In fact, studentized residuals and studentized deleted residuals measure the degree to which an observation is considered an outlier. Given a normal distribution, an outlier can be identified when the range of expected residuals become greater than the absolute value of 1.75 (See Muller, 1986).

Statistical Model Specifications

Two major categories of statistical techniques will be applied in this study: (1) pooled cross-sectional time-series analysis using pooled data, i.e., using "nation-year" as unit of analysis; and (2) ordinary least squares (OLS) or weighted least squares (WLS) regression analysis using cross-sectional data, i.e., using "nation" as unit of analysis. In the following sections, I discuss critical issues involving both methods of analysis. In addition, I describe the procedures used to carry out these two designs.

Introduction

Pooled cross-sectional time-series analysis is becoming more popular in various fields of social science research. Among the most popular introductory materials on the subject, there are Kmenta (1971, 1988), Maddala (1971), Stimson (1985), Judge et al. (1988) and Sayrs (1989). I use pooled cross-sectional time-series analysis as the major statistical technique in the current study for the following reasons: (1) pooled data are arrayed across both cross-sectionally differentiated entities such as nations and temporally differentiated ones like years. Intersections of time and space such as the "nation-year" serve as the units of analysis. The nation-year definition of pooled observation can greatly relax the 'small-N" problem (see Judge et al., 1988, chapter 11); (2) pooled data analysis permits inquiry into variables that elude study in simple cross-sectional or time-series arrays because their variability is negligible, or nonexistent across either time or space. This type of analysis permits systematic comparisons of cross-sectionally and longitudinally varying causal forces; (3) the use of pooled data also "permits cross-national shifts in statistical parameters and underlying changes in causal process to be studied in terms of temporally invariant traits of nations or cross-sectionally stolid characteristics of periods" (Hicks, 1994).

Problems Using OLS On Pooled Data

According to Hicks (1994:172), simply applying ordinary least squares (OLS) regression to pooled data suffers from the problem that errors for regression equations estimates tend to (1) be temporally autoregressive, i.e., errors are interdependent from one time period to the next; (2) be cross-sectionally heteroskedastic, i.e., the variances of the error terms are not constant across subsets of nations; (3) be cross-sectionally correlated, i.e., errors are correlated across nations; (4) have obscure unit and period effects, i.e., errors have both temporal and cross-sectional components which reflect both temporal period effects and cross-sectional unit effects; and (5) reflect some causal heterogeneity cross space, time, or both, i.e., errors may also tend to be non-random across space and time.

Two Pooled Cross-Sectional Time-Series Models

Two major models of pooled regression suggested by Judge et al. (1988, chapter 11) will be examined and selectively employed in this study. The first model is called "pooling time-series and cross-sectional data using dummy variables" which introduces dummy variables and estimates the parameters by OLS. Judge et al., (1988) write this model as:

$$Y_{it} = B_{1i} + \Sigma B_k X_{kit} + e_{it} \qquad [6]$$

or

$$Y_{it} = B_{1j} D_{jt} + \Sigma B_k X_{kit} + e_{it} \qquad [7]$$

where i and j = 1, 2, ..., N and t =1, 2, ..., T. D_{jt} are dummy variables and take values of 0 or 1. D_{jt} equal to 1 if j equals i and 0 if j not equal i. B_{1i} is the intercept coefficient for the ith cross-sectional unit. B_k represents the slope coefficients that are common to all individuals. Y_{it} is the dependent variable, the X_{kit} are the explanatory variables. e_{it} are independent and identically distributed random variables with $E[e_{it}] = o$ and $E[e] = \sigma_e^2$.

The second model is called the "pooling time-series and cross-sectional data using error components" which assumes a random intercept to give an error (or variance) components model that can be estimated by generalized least squares (GLS). Judge et al. (1988) write this model as:

$$Y_{it} = B_{1i} + \Sigma B_k X_{kit} + e_{it} \qquad [8]$$

or

$$Y_{it} = \overline{B}_1 + \Sigma B_k X_{kit} + \mu_i + e_{it} \qquad [9]$$

Notice that equation 8 appears to be the same as equation 6. Their underlying assumptions, however, are quite different. In equation 6 I assume that B_{1i} are fixed coefficients. In equation 8 I assume that they are independent random variables with a mean $\overline{B}_1$ and variance σ_μ^2. Thus, I can write

$$B_{1i} = \overline{B}_1 + \mu_i$$

where $E[\mu_i] = 0$, $E[\mu_i^2] = \sigma_\mu^2$ and $E[\mu_i \mu_j] = 0$ for $i \neq j$. It is also assumed that the μ_i are uncorrelated with e_{jt}, i.e., $E[\mu_i e_{jt}] = 0$. The definitions of Y_{it}, X_{kit} and e_{it} in equation 8 and 9 are the same as those defined in equation 6 and 7.

Choice Between Pooling Models: Dummy Variables vs. Error Components

Judge et al. (1988:489-90) provide a short discussion on the choice of model for pooling. In summary, two important aspects need to be addressed. First, one should be concerned about the relative sizes of N and T. When T is large and N is small, there is little difference between parameters estimated based on either model. When N is large and T is small, the parameter estimations can differ significantly. Taylor (1980) suggests that error components model using generalized least squares (GLS) estimation is more appropriate when (1) T is equal to or greater than 3 and N - K is equal to or greater than 9, and (2) T is equal to or greater than 2 and N - K is equal to or greater than 10.

Second, one should always consider the distinction between conditional or unconditional inference. Conditional inference based on the estimations from a dummy variable model is appropriate when the individuals, e.g., nations, on which I have data are not randomly drawn from the population, or when I am particularly interested in those individuals. On the contrary, when the individuals in the sample are randomly drawn from the population, or one is more interested in inferences about the population, unconditional inference that is implicit in the error components model is appropriate.

Implications

Data Structure, Diagnoses and Treatment

As discussed previously, I constructed two different data sets to facilitate my analysis: (1) cross-sectional data file; and (2) pooled data file. In the cross-sectional data file, I break the 25-year period (1960-1984) into five consecutive time periods: 1960-1964, 1965-1969, 1970-1974, 1975-1979, and 1980-1984. I will run separate cross-sectional analyses using either Ordinary Least Squares (OLS) or Weighted Least Squares (WLS) depending on diagnostic statistics. By using cross-sectional data, I intend to provide some contrasts and comparisons between the pooling method and the traditional cross-sectional regression design in testing my theoretical perspectives. I will use the five year averages of both the dependent variables and independent variables in the cross-sectional design. Using the pooled data, I will test the proposed theoretical models applying both the Ordinary Least Squares (OLS) and Least Square Dummy Variable (LSDV) techniques.

To address problems such as the erratic data reporting, heteroskedasticity, sample selection bias, missing data as well as influential cases, I will rely on a set of diagnostic techniques. First, I will run basic descriptive statistics to examine closely the distribution of variables in both the cross-sectional and the pooled data. Second, I will compare these descriptive statistics between two sub-sample groups: developed nations and developing nations. Given the fact that developed nations in general have better statistical systems and thus have less missing data problems, I pay special attention to discovering the possible patterns of missing data problems by comparing these two sub-sample groups. Third, I single out my dependent variables, i.e., homicide and theft, and measure the magnitude of their missing data problems for each of the five time periods involved. I hope this examination will contribute to my knowledge of the possible sample selection bias in the current study.

Fourth, Park's test of heteroskedasticity will be used to test whether a suspected factor such as the predicted probability of missing crime statistics has contributed to the changing variance of the error terms. If I can reject the null hypothesis of homoskedasticity, I will pursue Weighted Least Squares (WLS) procedure. If not, I will keep using Ordinary Least Squares (OLS) estimation. Fifth, Berk's (1983) correction procedure for sample selection bias will be followed. Separate logistic regression models will be run using dummy endogenous variables indicating whether there are missing data in homicide or theft for each of the time periods. Hazard rate instrument variables are constructed based on the saved predicted probabilities of nonresponses. These hazard rate instrument variables will then be added back to each of the substantive equations. Ordinary Least Squares (OLS) regression model including the hazard rate variable will be run to see whether the hazard rate has affected the regression coefficients of other explanatory variables or the intercept.

Guidelines for Choosing Between Different Analytical Tools Using Pooled Data

Since I do not have a randomly selected sample in this study, I am not trying to make unconditional inferences about the population; i.e., all nations in the world. I am, in fact, more interested in exploring country specific information and in discussing the similarities or dissimilarities among categories of nations. For example, it will be of great interest to us to examine whether the theories under discussion are equally applicable to developing nations as well as to the developed nations.

My pooled data structure using country-year as unit of analysis yields a substantially larger number of observations than is possible with either individual country time-series or cross-national analyses. As discussed previously, the OLS technique is applicable for this pooled data structure. OLS parameter estimators are unbiased and consistent but not efficient. There are a number of solutions available to improve the non-efficient OLS estimations: 1) Kmenta's Generalized Least Squares (GLS) estimation; 2) the Generalized Least Squares Error Components (GLSE) estimation and 3) the Least Squares Dummy Variable (LSDV) estimation.

I chose to run the LSDV model rather than the other two options for the current study for the following reasons. First, the examination of my data shows that the cross-sectional units (nations) differ significantly in the level of the dependent variables. A list of nations at the 0 (minimum), 25, 50, 75 and 100 (maximum) percentiles as well as the extreme values is provided in Table 2 to see the variation of the values of the dependent variables. I find that there are indeed significant variations in the levels of my dependent variables. The skewness scores also indicate the skewed distribution of the data. This gives us a hint that assuming a common intercept for all the nations may not be appropriate. Second, the Least Square Dummy Variable (LSDV) model allows intercepts to vary across nations by specified N-1 dummy variables for all the nations included in the sample. The intercept dummies are thus expected to capture the unmeasured factors that are cross-nationally variant but temporally invariant. This is of special interest to the current

Table 2: Percentile Distribution: Between-Country Differences in the Level of Dependent Variables, Homicide and Theft.[1]

	Minimum	25%	50%	75%	Maximum	Skewness
Homicide	.41 (Netherlands)	1.98 (Morocco)	3.19 (Australia)	8.19 (France)	32.81 (Burma)	2.76
Theft	14.45 (Philippines)	147.27 (Indonesia)	305.22 (Malawi)	1026.41 (Austria)	3393.71 (Sweden)	1.53

Extreme Values

	5 Highest		5 Lowest	
	Nation			Nation
Homicide	32.81	Burma	.41	Netherlands
	12.93	Jamaica	.42	Brunei
	12.80	Kuwait	.73	Spain
	11.69	USA	.82	New Zealand
	11.39	Italy	.88	Norway
Theft	3393.71	Sweden	14.45	Philippines
	2992.05	USA	46.18	Turkey
	2834.03	Germany	46.90	Syria
	2735.03	UK	65.74	Nigeria
	2322.69	Denmark	68.48	Peru

[1] Average scores for both homicide and theft were calculated based on all the available values covering the 25 year period of 1960 to 1984 for each of the nations in the sample. For example, for a nation with complete records of homicide and theft, the average scores for that nation are calculated as:

$$AVE\_HOM = (H60 + H61 + \ldots + H84) / 25$$
$$AVE\_THF = (T60 + T61 + \ldots + T84) / 25$$

research. Third, the Generalized Least Squares models--either the Kmenta model or error components model have the unique advantages of deriving more efficient estimation by correcting for autocorrelation and so on. Both of these two approaches, however, entail a loss of cross-national information by either assuming a common intercept or assuming the intercept as a random variable. Fourth, for the current study, I am particularly interested in getting information to answer questions raised by previous studies with regard to the differences between developed and developing nations, between core and periphery/semi-periphery nations. Thus, the LSDV model seems to be the preferable choice here.

Chapter VI

Research Results of the Cross-Sectional and Pooled Cross-Sectional Time-Series Analyses

Descriptive Statistics

Cross-Sectional Data

    1) For the Entire Sample

    Table 3 has the distributions of the means, standard deviations and total number of cases for variables involved in the analysis divided into five time periods. Using cross-sectional data set in which nations are the unit of analysis, I calculated the 5-year averages for each of the variables included in the analysis for each of the five time periods. The means for the rates of homicide across all five time periods are relatively stable, ranging from the low value 5.25 per 100,000 population (1970-1974) to the high value of 6.12 per 100, 000 population (1980-1984). The means for the rates of theft show greater variation and generally a growth pattern across the five time periods. The data indicate that the theft rates for the first three time periods, i.e., 1960-1964, 1965-1969 and 1970-1974 are much lower compared to the later two time periods, 1975-1979 and 1980-1984. Meanwhile, the standard deviation scores

Table 3:   Descriptive Statistics: Cross-Sectional Data and Comparisons Between Developed and Developing Nations.

	60-64			65-69			70-74			75-79			80-84		
	Mean	Std.	N	Mean	Std.	N	Mean	Std.	N	Mean	Std.	N	Mean	Std.	N
HOMICIDE	5.40	6.39	43	5.73	5.73	46	5.25	5.42	40	5.97	4.50	23	6.12	7.47	20
- Developed	3.28	4.01	19	4.29	4.12	19	4.05	4.66	16	4.89	4.15	16	3.37	1.89	14
- Developing	7.08	7.44	24	6.74	6.52	27	6.05	5.83	24	8.43	4.85	7	12.55	11.49	6
LNHOMIC	1.00	1.35	43	1.43	.78	46	1.15	1.11	40	1.50	.80	23	1.31	.96	20
- Developed	.36	1.50	19	1.13	.78	19	.70	1.34	16	1.29	.79	16	1.07	.56	14
- Developing	1.51	.97	24	1.64	.72	27	1.46	.84	24	1.98	.62	7	1.89	1.44	6
THEFT	391.40	418.60	45	466.90	581.60	47	582.80	756.30	38	1534.00	1610.60	32	1957.20	2106.90	26
- Developed	538.03	517.21	19	665.86	681.99	20	967.17	873.77	14	2198.96	1660.35	19	2957.53	2136.75	16
- Developing	284.30	295.86	26	319.57	453.48	27	358.55	588.44	24	562.17	918.22	13	356.66	309.27	10
LNTHEFT	5.36	1.27	45	5.38	1.39	47	5.54	1.47	38	6.61	1.36	32	6.66	1.74	26
- Developed	5.68	1.27	19	5.77	1.46	20	6.40	1.09	14	7.27	1.10	19	7.57	1.12	16
- Developing	5.13	1.23	26	5.08	1.29	27	5.04	1.46	24	5.65	1.13	13	5.20	1.59	10
SURPLUS	141.80	56.30	34	151.90	80.50	38	149.30	85.60	40	131.40	73.90	39	125.30	67.90	35
- Developed	113.71	37.71	19	104.94	33.91	19	94.72	33.86	19	81.06	26.59	19	92.01	35.77	19
- Developing	177.44	56.60	15	198.77	86.67	19	198.58	88.73	21	179.28	72.92	20	164.89	76.51	16
UNEMP	3.44	2.80	18	3.93	3.72	25	3.79	4.11	25	5.49	4.42	29	7.33	5.30	29
- Developed	2.42	1.80	13	2.25	1.11	14	2.48	1.42	15	4.51	2.17	18	7.13	4.08	18
- Developing	6.10	3.39	5	6.06	4.76	11	5.77	5.89	10	7.09	6.49	11	7.65	7.09	11

Table 3 (cont.)

	60-64			65-69			70-74			75-79			80-84		
	Mean	Std.	N	Mean	Std.	N	Mean	Std.	N	Mean	Std.	N	Mean	Std.	N
GOVEXP	45.61	18.18	16	44.61	16.66	22	42.20	16.26	31	42.15	15.14	25	43.27	14.27	24
- Developed	45.57	16.47	11	48.07	16.41	12	48.68	14.84	16	48.33	10.39	14	49.32	11.12	14
- Developing	45.68	23.69	5	40.46	16.84	10	35.29	15.20	15	34.27	16.96	11	34.78	14.31	10
URBAN	22.63	25.55	48	20.28	25.25	48	21.12	23.48	48	18.37	22.29	48	19.92	25.25	48
- Developed	36.46	26.22	20	33.03	27.52	20	33.59	26.73	20	24.86	22.13	20	29.26	26.31	20
- Developing	12.75	20.25	28	11.18	19.26	28	12.21	16.11	28	13.73	21.61	28	14.84	23.64	28
INDUS	.20	.11	34	.19	.10	41	.19	.09	45	.19	.08	45	.19	.07	44
- Developed	.29	.07	17	.29	.06	18	.27	.06	19	.25	.05	19	.23	.05	19
- Developing	.11	.06	17	.13	.06	23	.14	.06	26	.15	.07	26	.15	.07	25
GROW_1	90.87	84.92	38	38.41	62.19	43	306.10	333.81	46	572.32	838.19	47	6.77	364.64	46
- Developed	157.30	68.36	17	79.02	30.17	17	530.43	204.01	19	774.82	385.99	19	53.56	429.41	18
- Developing	37.09	53.06	21	11.86	63.73	26	148.25	318.42	27	434.91	1024.31	28	-23.31	321.11	28
MORAL	-	-	-	-	-	-	-	-	-	7.58	3.78	46	7.86	3.77	46
- Developed	-	-	-	-	-	-	-	-	-	11.12	1.46	19	11.46	.75	19
- Developing	-	-	-	-	-	-	-	-	-	5.09	2.77	27	5.32	2.82	27
DEMOC	6.49	4.01	44	6.11	4.32	44	5.40	4.52	44	-	-	-	-	-	-
- Developed	8.58	3.22	19	8.38	3.46	19	8.32	3.73	19	-	-	-	-	-	-
- Developing	4.90	3.86	25	4.39	4.16	25	3.18	3.80	25	-	-	-	-	-	-

Table 3 (cont.)

	60-64			65-69			70-74			75-79			80-84		
	Mean	Std.	N	Mean	Std.	N	Mean	Std.	N	Mean	Std.	N	Mean	Std.	N
FLABOR	32.43	26.36	48	29.59	24.66	48	29.45	23.88	48	27.10	22.58	48	29.03	24.47	48
- Developed	47.11	20.84	20	42.18	22.37	20	40.96	25.39	20	35.06	24.43	20	37.40	24.74	20
- Developing	21.94	25.11	28	20.60	22.48	28	21.22	19.26	28	21.42	19.68	28	23.05	22.86	28
DIVORCE	4.34	1.64	48	4.42	1.59	48	4.52	1.79	48	4.34	1.72	48	4.40	1.70	48
- Developed	3.94	1.89	20	3.55	1.39	20	4.54	1.83	20	4.13	1.21	20	4.02	1.76	20
- Developing	4.63	1.39	28	5.04	1.44	28	4.51	1.79	28	4.50	2.02	28	4.67	1.64	28
POP_1	5.6E+5	1.6E+6	47	5.3E+5	1.6E+6	48	6.0E+5	1.7E+6	49	6.7E+5	1.9E+6	49	8.0E+5	2.8E+6	49
- Developed	3.7E+5	6.5E+5	20	3.4E+5	5.4E+5	20	2.8E+5	4.7E+5	20	2.8E+5	6.2E+5	20	2.3E+5	5.3E+5	20
- Developing	7.1E+5	2.0E+6	27	6.7E+5	2.1E+6	28	8.1E+5	2.2E+6	29	9.5E+5	2.4E+6	29	1.2E+6	3.5E+6	29

* Developed Nations (n =20).

** Developing Nations (n =29).

for both homicide and theft are almost always greater than their mean scores. This indicates possible skewed distribution of the data. I proceed to use log transformation for both of my dependent variables (LNHOMIC and LNTHEFT). The relevant statistics are also reported in Table 3.

In addition to the dependent variables, Table 3 reveals detailed information of the explanatory variables. I find that there is not much variation in mean scores for some of my explanatory variables across the five time periods. For example, the means for the government expenditure variable (GOVEXP) range from the lowest of 42.15 (1975-1979) to the highest of 45.61 (1960-1964). The means for urbanization (URBAN) range from 18.37 (1975-1979) to 22.63 (1960-1964). Similar patterns are also observed in other variables such as industrialization (INDUS), moral individualism (MORAL), female labor force participation (FLABOR), and divorce (DIVORCE). There are, however, a few exceptions. First of all, there appears to be a pattern of increase for the mean scores of unemployment (UNEMP) which takes the lowest value of 3.44 for the 1960 to 1964 period but the highest value of 7.33 for the time period of 1980 to 1984. A similar pattern of increase is also found for population growth (POP_1) which has the lowest mean of 560,000 (1960-1964) and the highest mean of 800,000 (1980-1984). Secondly, there is a declining trend for the mean scores of surplus value (SURPLUS) from the highest of 151.9 (1965-1969) to the lowest of 125.3 (1980-1984). Third, the variable of economic growth (GROWTH_1) has the most variation in its mean score values, especially for the two time periods in the 1970s when the means scores are much higher than those observed for other time periods.

It is certainly legitimate for one to question whether the construction of the sample has affected the distribution of the means and standard deviations of the variables. Because of the missing data problem, I might not be able to retain the same number of cases (nations) as listed in Table 1 for each of the five time periods. As a result, for some time periods, it is possible that there are more developed nations or developing nations in the sample and the descriptive statistics calculated based on their values are no longer representative for the entire sample. I argue that the sample selection problem may have a profound impact on the descriptive as well as on bivariate and multivariate analysis. Although I will apply formal statistical test to address the sample selection bias problem in the subsequent section, I start with comparisons of the detailed descriptive statistics between the developed and the developing nation sub-samples.

2) Developed vs. Developing Nations

In Table 3 I provide comparative descriptive statistics for two sub-sample groups: developed and developing nations in the cross-sectional data. It can be easily observed that there are great between-sample variations in means, standard deviations as well as in the magnitude of missing data. The divorce rate (DIVORCE) is probably the only variable for which no clear pattern of difference between the developed and developing nations was found. The means of the divorce rate for both sub-sample groups remain fairly stable throughout the five time periods from 1960 to 1984.

The following represent patterns of differences between the two sub-samples. First, developing nations have consistently higher homicide rates and lower theft rates across all five time periods compared to those of the developed nations. Second, the means of surplus value, unemployment, and population growth for the developing nation sub-sample are consistently greater than those found in the developed nation sub-sample. Third, compared to the developing nations, the developed nations are more urbanized and industrialized. Collectively, developed nations score much higher on the scales of moral individualism and democracy. Developed nations also have higher female labor force participation rates and, there are greater percentages of government expenditures allocated to social welfare, health and education in developed nations.

3) Differential Attrition of Samples

There are some solutions for the missing data problem when it only exists in the independent variables. However, it is not unusual in comparative research that one encounters the problem of missing data in the dependent variable. In a cross-national data set in which nations are the units of analysis, having missing values for the dependent variable usually means the exclusion of this case entirely from the analysis. Although I have used five-year average scores for my dependent variables to enhance the reliability of the crime statistics (measures of homicide and theft rates) and to boost the sample size, I still anticipate a potential problem of differential attrition in sample sizes across the five time periods. Table 4 provides the first look at the differential attrition issue in my case.

Compared to Table 1 in which the full sample for the study was included (N=49), different proportions of cases have to be excluded in individual analyses because of the missing data problem for the dependent variables. Generally speaking, case attrition is less severe in the three earlier time periods: 1960-1964, 1965-1969 and 1970-1974 for the analyses involving both homicide and theft. Also, developed nations are more likely to be retained in the sample. I should point it out that in the two later time periods--1975-1979 and 1980-1984--more than half of the developing nations in the original sample were excluded. Therefore, the number of cases available for analysis decreased dramatically. Developed nations are the dominating force in the remaining samples representing the later two time periods.

Pooled Data

Table 5 provides descriptive statistics for the pooled data in which nation-year is the unit of analysis. Notice that I present the pooled data in two longer time periods in this table. The first time period covers the 15-year period of 1960 to 1974. The second covers the 10-year period of 1975 to 1984.

There are several reasons for doing so. First of all, I have used two different data sources for the analysis of the entire 25-year period of 1960 to 1984. I use Archer and Gartner's Comparative Crime Data File (CCDF) for my dependent variables for the first 15 years, i.e., 1960 to 1974. I use the United Nations' 2nd and 3rd World Crime Survey (WCS) for the latter period, i.e., 1975 to 1984. Combining

Table 4:   Differential Case Attrition Due to Missing Data in Dependent Variables.

| | Number and Percentage of Cases Missing[1] | | |
	Total Sample (N = 49)	Developed Nations (n = 20)	Developing Nations (n = 29)
	Homicide		
1960-1964	6 (12.2%)	1 (5%)	5 (17.2%)
1965-1969	3 (6.1%)	1 (5%)	2 (6.9%)
1970-1974	9 (18.4%)	4 (20%)	5 (17.2%)
1975-1979	26 (53.1%)	4 (20%)	22 (75.9%)
1980-1984	29 (59.2%)	6 (30%)	23 (79.3%)
	Theft		
1960-1964	4 (8.2%)	1 (5%)	3 (10.3%)
1965-1969	2 (4.1%)	0 (0%)	2 (6.9%)
1970-1974	11 (22.4%)	6 (30%)	5 (17.2%)
1975-1979	17 (34.7%)	1 (5%)	16 (55.2%)
1980-1984	23 (46.9%)	4 (20%)	19 (65.5%)

[1] For a case to be excluded from analysis for any of the 5-year time periods, data have to be missing for all five years in that period.

Table 5:   Descriptive Statistics of Pooled Data.

	1960-1974			1975-1984		
	Mean	SD	N	Mean	SD	N
HOMICID	6.11	6.40	501	6.96	6.25	198
LNHOM.	1.45	.82	501	1.67	.69	198
THEFT	471.55	577.74	499	1758.01	1846.15	280
LNTHEFT	5.39	1.39	499	6.65	1.54	280
SURPLUS	139.24	71.49	484	122.54	68.31	349
UNEMP	3.53	3.13	294	6.50	5.17	274
GOVEXP	41.99	15.77	242	42.82	14.74	221
URBAN	21.43	28.52	621	19.18	27.65	411
INDUS	.20	.10	425	.19	.08	420
GROW_1	161.55	367.33	531	245.98	1038.73	398
MORAL	-	-	-	8.72	3.82	460
DEMOC	5.93	4.30	660	-	-	-
FLABOR	30.55	29.81	600	28.09	28.01	400
DIVORCE	4.43	3.07	549	4.38	3.03	335
POP_1	5.3E+5	1.6E+6	647	7.4E+5	2.6E+6	488

the two data sources in any single analysis of the entire 25-year period requires the assumption that any variations in the rates of homicide and theft are genuine rather than caused by differences in measurement. Second, based on the examination of the cross-section data in Table 2 and Figure 4, it seems reasonable and safer to split the 25-year time period into two. In general, the rates of homicide and theft for the first 15-year period are lower than the following 10-year period, much more so the case for the unlogged theft rate.

Third, the subsequent analysis using Least Square Dummy Variable (LSDV) technique assumes the unmeasured factors to be cross-nationally variant but temporally invariant. Logically, the latter assumption can be met easier when the time period is shorter.

Compared to the cross-sectional data in Table 3, the pooled data in Table 5 have fewer missing data problems. Instead of using average scores of variables for each of the five time periods in the cross-sectional data, my pooled data use all the available nation-year information for each variables. It is observable that there are differences for both the dependent and the independent variables between the two time periods, i.e., 1960-1974 and 1975-1984.

The means of homicide for each of the two pooled time periods remain in the range of 6 to 7 per 100,000 population. The means for theft, however, appear to be at two different levels. For the first 15-year time period (1960-1974), the mean theft rate was about 472 per 100,000 population. But, for the second 10-year period (1975-1984), the mean theft rate was about 1,758 per 100,000 population, a dramatic increase. Both dependent variables are log transformed due to the observed skewness in their distributions.

The means for the following variables are stable in the two pooled time periods: government expenditure (GOVEXP), urbanization (URBAN), industrialization (INDUS), female labor force participation (FLABOR) and divorce (DIVORCE). Unemployment (UNEMP), economic growth (GROWTH_1), and population growth (POP_1) are the three variables which show a general increase

Figure 4
Average Rate of Homicide and Theft by Time Period

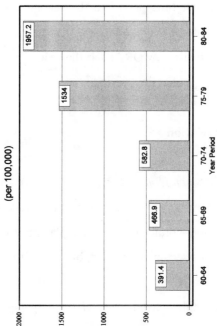

Theft Rates
(per 100,000)

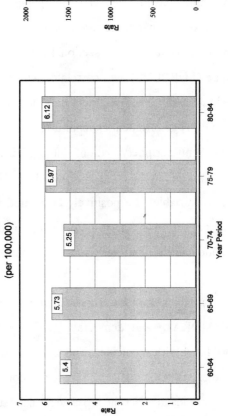

Homicide Rates
(per 100,000)

trend from the first time period to the second. The mean of the surplus value (SURPLUS) variable appears to be lower at the second time period. The mean score for moral individualism (MORAL) at the second pooled time period is higher than it was at the first pooled time period.[2]

Bivariate Correlation

Correlations Between Homicide and the Explanatory Variables

Table 6 displays the results of the zero-order correlations between the dependent variable-homicide, and the explanatory variables for each of the 5 time periods in the cross-sectional data, and for each of the two time periods in the pooled data.

For variables from the Marxian perspective, I observed that (1) unemployment (UNEMP) has significant positive correlation with homicide in three of the five time periods in the cross-sectional data and in both pooled time periods; (2) surplus value (SURPLUS) also correlates with homicide positively in the two early time periods in the cross-sectional data and in the first pooled time period (1960-1974); and (3) government expenditure (GOVEXP), periphery nation status (PERIPH), and semi-periphery nation status (SEMIPERI) have no significant correlation with homicide in the cross-sectional data. However, periphery and semi-periphery dummy variables are positively correlated with homicide in the pooled data. The only exception is that in the second pooled time period, the correlation between homicide and the semi-periphery status dummy variable is not statistically significant.

For the variables from the Durkheimian perspective, I found that (1) moral individualism (MORAL) and democracy (DEMOC) are both consistently and negatively correlated with homicide. The signs of correlation are in the predicted direction; (2) there is no statistically significant correlation between urbanization (URBAN) and homicide in either the cross-sectional data or the pooled data; and (3)

Table 6:   Pearsons Correlations Between Homicide Rate and Each of the
             Independent Variables by Data Type.

| | | | HOMICIDE | | | | |
| | Cross-Sectional Data | | | | | Pooled Data | |
	60-64	65-69	70-74	75-79	80-84	60-74	75-84
UNEMP	.247*	.178	.260*	.196	.541*	.237*	.358*
SURPLUS	.372*	.312*	.122	.039	.001	.228*	.069
GOVEXP	-.114	-.121	-.092	.104	.005	-.043	.020
PERIPH	.050	.044	-.011	.207	.440	.089*	.286*
SEMIPERI	.190	.177	.110	.119	-.158	.145*	.081
URBAN	-.049	.005	.149	.099	.042	-.034	-.001
INDUS	-.155	-.269*	-.097	-.029	-.274	-.147*	-.181*
GROWTH_1	-.216	-.214*	-.287*	.035	-.579*	.001	-.164*
MORAL	-	-	-	-.220	-.386*	-	-.335*
DEMOC	-.308*	-.104	-.291*	-	-	-.226*	-
DIVORCE	.203*	.238*	.107	-.343*	.239	.116*	.013
FLABOR	-.215	-.095	-.026	.019	-.218	-.172*	-.103*
POP_1	.029	.035	.056	.274	.153	-.098*	.159*

* $p < .05$.

the statistically significant correlations between either industrialization (INDUS) and homicide, or between economic growth (GROWTH_1) and homicide are not in the predicted direction.

For the control variables, divorce rates (DIVORCE) in the two early time periods (1960-1964, 1965-1969) in cross-sectional data and in the first pooled time period (1960-1974) are positively correlated with homicide. The correlation between divorce rate and homicide is negative for the time period of 1975-1979. Secondly, neither female labor force participation (FLABOR) nor population growth (POP_1) is correlated with homicide significantly in the cross-sectional data. Nevertheless, both are significantly correlated with homicide in the pooled data.

Correlations Between Theft and Explanatory Variables

Table 7 presents the results of the zero-order correlations between the dependent variable-theft, and the explanatory variables in both the cross-sectional data and the pooled data.

For the Marxian perspective in both the cross-sectional and pooled data time periods, I observed that (1) unemployment rate (UNEMP), surplus value (SURPLUS), periphery (PERIPH) and semi-periphery (SEMIPERI) status dummy variables are negatively correlated with theft. However, they are in the opposite directions of those predicted in the earlier hypotheses; and (2) the correlations between government expenditure (GOVEXP) and theft rate are positive. They are contrary to the predicted directions.

For the Durkheimian perspective in both the cross-sectional and the pooled data time periods, the correlations between theft and each of the following variables are positive and mostly significant: urbanization (URBAN), industrialization (INDUS) and economic growth (GROWTH_1). They are all in the predicted directions. The only exception are the correlations between moral individualism (MORAL) and theft. They are significantly positively correlated, contrary to my prediction.

Table 7:   Pearsons Correlations Between Theft Rate and Each of the Independent Variables by Data Type.

	THEFT						
	Cross-Sectional Data					Pooled Data	
	60-64	65-69	70-74	75-79	80-84	60-74	75-84
UNEMP	-.275*	-.121	-.097	-.083	.072	-.309*	.057
SURPLUS	-.298*	-.244*	-.359*	-.610*	-.640*	-.281*	-.580*
GOVEXP	.079	.202	.104	.335*	.338*	.165*	.335*
PERIPH	-.095	-.144	-.222*	-.291*	-.391*	-.159*	-.315*
SEMIPERI	-.095	-.050	-.159	-.299*	-.218	-.084*	-.264*
URBAN	.187	.259*	.300*	.088	.136	.243*	.111*
INDUS	.264*	.252*	.320*	.172	.510*	.287*	.314*
GROWTH_1	.404*	.168	.339*	.379*	.122	.010*	.214*
MORAL	-	-	-	.722*	.739*	-	.710*
DEMOC	.281*	.380*	.431*	-	-	.377*	-
DIVORCE	-.167	.075	-.047	-.041	-.350*	-.019	-.099*
FLABOR	.141	.206	.175	.148	.186	.164*	.169*
POP_1	-.166	-.143	-.217*	-.280*	-.246	.011	-.231*

* $p < .05$.

For the control variables, divorce rate (DIVORCE) is negatively correlated with theft in only two time periods: 1980-1984 in cross-sectional data, and 1975-1984 in the pooled data. Female labor force participation (FLABOR) is not significantly correlated with theft in the cross-sectional data but is positively correlated with theft in the pooled data. Population growth (POP_1) is negatively correlated with theft in two time periods in the cross-sectional data, i.e., 1970-1974 and 1975-1979 and one time period in the pooled data, i.e., 1975-1984.

Brief Summary and Discussion

A few characteristics of the bivariate correlation analysis can be summarized. First, predicted and unpredicted bivariate correlations between crime rates (homicide and theft) and the explanatory variables from both theoretical perspectives were found. Second, the observed correlations are not consistent across all time periods involved in the test. Third, it appears that hypotheses generated based on each of the two perspectives are sensitive to types of crime. For example, hypotheses based on the Marxian perspective for homicide are more likely to be supported than those based on the Durkheimian perspective. On the other hand, hypotheses based on the Durkheimian perspective for theft are more likely to be supported than those based on the Marxian perspective.

In the past three decades, criminologists have been debating whether there is really a single "cause" that produces both homicide and theft. Much of the existing research, however, does not include both homicide and theft in the same study. Earlier research that included both homicide and property crimes in the same study failed to find a common cause for both types of crimes (Gurr et al., 1977; Hartnagel, 1982; Kick and LaFree, 1985; Krohn, 1976, 1978; Krohn and Wellford, 1977; McDonald, 1976; Wellford, 1974; Wolf, 1971). Although comparative criminology has made some progress in the past decades, comparative criminologists have not been able to develop precise specifications of the processes causing different crimes (Neuman and Berger, 1988:290). I argue that the major obstacles in providing more precise specifications are (1) a lack of theoretical exercise; and (2) methodological complications. Therefore, it is reasonable that I systematically take into consideration some of the more intriguing methodological issues in the cross-national testing of theoretical perspectives. It is for this very reason that I incorporate the following important diagnostic tests before I start my multivariate analysis.

Diagnostic Statistics

As proposed in the preceding chapter, three types of diagnostic statistics are used to provide guidance for further analyses. First, I present the logit results with regard to the issue of sample selection bias. Second, I test whether the saved predicted probabilities of having missing data in dependent variables (from logit analysis) contribute significantly to the variance of the error terms in the substantive regression equations by applying Park's test of heteroskedasticity.[3] Third, I display three types of residual statistics. I make suggestions for the subsequent statistical analyses according to the findings from each of the diagnostic procedure.

Using Logistic Regressions to Test Sample Selection Bias

Table 8 displays the logit estimates of the likelihood of missing homicide statistics across all time periods using both the cross-sectional and the pooled data. Table 9 reports the logit estimates of likelihood of missing theft statistics across all time periods in both the cross-sectional and the pooled data. For the purpose of the current discussion, I include only a few types of statistics from the logistic regression outputs. I report the logistic regression coefficients, the standard errors, pseudo R squared and the total number of cases involved in the logit analysis.

1) Logit Results Using the Cross-Sectional Data

I found that the following observations are applicable to both Table 8 and Table 9 (1) surplus value (SURPLUS) has an positive effect on the likelihood of missing crime statistics (homicide or theft) for the 1975-1979 time period indicating that nations which generate higher surplus values are more likely to have missing

Table 8:   Missing Homicide Statistics Regressed on Key Variables: Logistic Regression Coefficients (Standard Errors in Parentheses).

HOMICIDE (Dummy)[1]

	Cross-Sectional Data (N = 49)					Pooled Data (N_1=735; N_2=490)	
	1960-64	1965-69	1970-74	1975-79	1980-84	1960-74	1975-84
	b	b	b	b	b	b	b
Marxian:							
UNEMP	-.276 (.387)	-.000 (.286)	-.307 (.434)	.219 (.193)	.051 (.089)	.025 (.042)	.052 (.029)
SURPLUS	.005 (.010)	.004 (.009)	.008 (.006)	.017* (.008)	.013 (.009)	.003 (.002)	.010* (.003)
GOVEXP	-.043 (.059)	-.015 (.057)	.023 (.034)	.005 (.036)	-.043 (.039)	-.013 (.010)	-.013 (.012)
SEMIPERI	1.396 (1.419)	-.267 (1.632)	-.877 (1.112)	1.814 (.971)	1.426 (.897)	.160 (.215)	1.850* (.286)
PERIPH	1.201 (1.509)	-.380 (1.969)	-.550 (1.372)	.622 (1.060)	1.049 (.905)	.359 (.234)	1.308* (.290)
Pseudo R^2	.045	.009	.075	.289*	.223*	.023*	.218*

Table 8 (cont.)

	Cross-Sectional Data (N = 49)					Pooled Data (N₁=735: N₂=490)	
	1960-64	1965-69	1970-74	1975-79	1980-84	1960-74	1975-84
	b	b	b	b	b	b	b
Durkheimian:							
GROWTH_1	.001 (.007)	.005 (.009)	.001 (.001)	-.000 (.000)	.000 (.000)	.002* (.000)	-.000 (.000)
INDUS	-.064 (.066)	-.038 (.087)	.014 (.069)	-.059 (.055)	-.013 (.054)	-.022 (.014)	-.027 (.016)
URBAN	-.021 (.034)	-.000 (.043)	.003 (.025)	.016 (.018)	.011 (.014)	-.003 (.004)	.013* (.005)
MORAL	- -	- -	- -	-.304* (.116)	-.279* (.112)	- -	-.266* (.034)
DEMOC	-.003 (.136)	-.189 (.194)	-.334* (.137)	- -	- -	-.117* (.023)	- -
Pseudo R²	.063	.050	.163*	.243*	.165*	.086*	.176*

[1] A dummy variable coded as 1 when homicide data is missing, 0 otherwise.
* p < .05, significance based on Wald Statistics.

crime data during the 1975-1979 time period; and (2) moral individualism (MORAL) and democracy (DEMOC) have consistent negative effect on the likelihood of missing crime statistics (homicide or theft) in three time periods--1970-1974, 1975-1979 and 1980-1984. This indicates that nations which scores lower on moral individualism and democracy are more likely to have missing crime statistics during these time periods.

2) Logit Results from the Pooled Data

For the two time periods involved in the pooled data, I observed that, first, for the earlier time period, i.e., 1960-1974, none of the Marxian explanatory variables had a significant effect on the likelihood of missing crime statistics; second, for the later time period, i.e., 1975-1984, however, surplus value (SURPLUS), Semi-periphery nation status (SEMIPERI) and Periphery nation status (PERIPH) all had significant positive effects on the likelihood of missing crime statistics while unemployment (UNEMP) had a significant positive effect on the likelihood of missing theft statistics for the 1975 to 1984 period; third, for the earlier time period, i.e., 1960-1974, two Durkheimian explanatory variables-economic growth (GROWTH_1) and democracy (DEMOC), had significant effects on the likelihood of missing crime statistics. Economic growth had significant positive effects and democracy had significant negative effects on the likelihood of missing crime statistics; and fourth, for the later time period, i.e., 1975-1984, urbanization (URBAN) had a significant positive effect on the likelihood of missing homicide statistics. Economic growth (GROWTH_1) had a significant negative effect on the likelihood of missing theft statistics. Additionally, moral individualism (MORAL) had significant negative effects on the likelihood of missing crime statistics.

3) Further Observations and Suggestions

A quick reference to Table 3-descriptive statistics and table 4-differential case attrition due to missing data in dependent variables reveals that (1) developing nations generate higher surplus values; (2) developing nations score consistently lower on both the moral individualism and the democracy scales; and (3) developing

Table 9: Missing Theft Statistics Regressed on Key Variables: Logistic Regression Coefficients (Standard Errors in Parentheses).

	Cross-Sectional Data (N=49)					Pooled Data (N_1 =735; N_2 =490)	
	1960-64 b	1965-69 b	1970-74 b	1975-79 b	1980-84 b	1960-74 b	1975-84 b
				THEFT (Dummy)[1]			
Marxian:							
UNEMP	-.240 (.442)	-.086 (.255)	-.049 (.214)	.140 (.110)	.016 (.081)	.025 (.041)	.057* (.026)
SURPLUS	.010 (.011)	-.011 (.016)	.009 (.006)	.024* (.009)	.011 (.007)	.002 (.002)	.013* (.002)
GOVEXP	-.034 (.064)	.021 (.154)	.023 (.032)	.055 (.042)	-.036 (.036)	-.014 (.010)	.014 (.011)
SEMIPERI	.636 (1.497)	.702 (1.506)	-1.778 (1.027)	1.733 (1.282)	1.450 (.856)	.000 (.214)	1.488* (.287)
PERIPH	.150 (1.728)	.114 (1.066)	-1.626 (1.275)	.619 (1.458)	.559 (.882)	.381 (.231)	.861* (.299)
Pseudo R^2	.033	.107	.097	.319*	.176	.019*	.189*

Table 9 (cont.)

	Cross-Sectional Data (N=49)					Pooled Data (N₁=735; N₂=490)	
	1960-64 b	1965-69 b	1970-74 b	1975-79 b	1980-84 b	1960-74 b	1975-84 b
Durkheimian:							
GROWTH_1	-.001 (.009)	.000 (.010)	.001 (.001)	-.000 (.000)	-.003* (.002)	.002* (.000)	-.003* (.001)
INDUS	-.109 (.088)	-.127 (.173)	.025 (.059)	-.089 (.057)	.023 (.055)	-.018 (.013)	-.029 (.016)
URBAN	-.026 (.053)	.122 (.071)	.014 (.021)	.001 (.017)	-.012 (.014)	.007 (.004)	-.005 (.004)
MORAL	- -	- -	- -	-.227* (.112)	-.257* (.111)	- -	-.214* (.031)
DEMOC	-.001 (.171)	-.821 (.713)	-.278* (.115)	- -	- -	-.122* (.023)	- -
Pseudo R²	.082	.133	.139	.220*	.226*	.074*	.169*

[1] A dummy variable coded as 1 when theft data is missing, 0 otherwise.

* p < .05, significance based on Wald Statistics.

nations have consistent higher percentages of missing values in both homicide and theft statistics compared to those of the developed nations. The formal test using logistic regressions partially confirms the general observations from the earlier descriptive statistics that, in some time periods, the remaining samples may no longer be representative for the original sample selection. It is likely that developing nations are excluded more frequently from analyses because of the missing data problem.

Based on my initial examination of the sample selection bias problem using logit analysis (reported in table 8 and table 9), I anticipate possible sample selection bias in my study. Berk 's (1983:235) general advice on the issue is to "proceed where possible with the corrections unless a strong argument can be made that moots the problem". Although significant indicators have been found, my logistic analyses results do not suggest that the possible sample selection bias is omnipresent in analyses involving all models and across all time periods, because some equations are not significant and even when they are, the pseudo R squared values are low.[4] Taking a conservative approach, I run a set of secondary logistic regressions using only those variables which have been found to have a significant effect on the predicted probabilities of missing crime statistics in the initial logit analysis. I then save the predicted probability of missing crime statistics from the secondary logistic regressions. I use them as the correction for sample selection bias. As a result, I create 14 hazard rate instrumental variables. These are later included in the substantive regression equations. Results with or without these correction factors are to be compared. Table 10 provides descriptive statistics for the hazard rate instrumental variables. I observe that the mean probabilities of missing homicide statistics are lower that those of missing theft statistics.

Researchers have suggested that more frequent absence of crime statistics may indicate greater measurement error (Messner, 1992). I wonder whether this measurement error in crime statistics will contribute to the variance of the error terms in regression analysis. To examine this possibility, I use the hazard rate instrument variables as the suspected proportionality factor in Park's test of heteroskedasticity.

Table 10:   Descriptive Statistics for Crime Hazard Rate Instrumental Variables by Theoretical Perspective and Time Period.[1]

	Marxian Perspective				Durkheimian Perspective			
	Mean	S.D.	Min.	Max.	Mean	S. D.	Min.	Max.
Homicide Dummy								
1960-1964	-	-	-	-	-	-	-	-
1965-1969	-	-	-	-	-	-	-	-
1970-1974	-	-	-	-	.18	.17	.033	.410
1975-1979	.53	.25	.168	.983	.53	.26	.213	.919
1980-1984	-	-	-	-	.59	.21	.343	.922
(N=49)								
1960-1974	-	-	-	-	.32	.14	.079	.997
1975-1984	.60	.25	.206	.968	.60	.22	.280	.949
(N=490)								
Theft Dummy								
1960-1964	-	-	-	-	-	-	-	-
1965-1969	-	-	-	-	-	-	-	-
1970-1974	-	-	-	-	.22	.14	.084	.415
1975-1979	.35	.27	.059	.962	.35	.22	.108	.763
1980-1984	-	-	-	-	.47	.25	.019	.989
(N=49)								
1960-1974	-	-	-	-	.32	.13	.089	.996
1975-1984	.43	.23	.088	.952	.43	.21	.068	.934
(N=490)								

[1] A total of 14 hazard rate instrument variables are constructed based on the predicted probabilities of missing observations in homicide and theft data for both theoretical perspectives.

Park's Test of Heteroskedasticity

Table 11 reports the results of Park's test of heteroskedasticity. I present the bivariate regression results using the logarithm of squared residual (LNE^2) as the dependent variable and the logarithm of the suspected proportionality factor Z (LNZ) as the independent variable.[5]

Cross-sectional Data

I can see that none of the unstandardized regression coefficient are statistically significant at the .05 level in the analyses using cross-sectional data. This means that there is no evidence that the suspected proportionality factor Z, the predicted probability of missing crime statistics, have contributed significantly to the variance of the error term. Thus, Park's test of heteroskedasticity does not give support to use weighted least square (WLS) estimation in analysis using cross-sectional data. Therefore, I will use ordinary least square regression in the subsequent analyses using the cross-sectional data.

Pooled Data

Using the pooled data, I found that there are four unstandardized regression coefficients that are significant at the .05 level as the result of Park's test. They came from the following regression models: (1) Marxian models on theft for both of the two pooled time periods, i.e., 1960-1974 and 1975-1984; and (2) Durkheimian models on both homicide and theft for the later pooled time period, 1975-1984. The results indicate that, in four occasions, the suspected proportionality factor Z, the probability of missing crime statistics, had significant impact on the variance of the error term. This violates one of basic regression assumptions that the variance of the error term should be constant. Therefore, I will use Weighted Least Squares (WLS) in addition to the Ordinary Least Squares (OLS) to estimate the above identified models. Results from both types of analysis are to be compared.

Table 11: Park's Test of Heteroskedasticity: Unstandardized Regression Coefficients from Bivariate Regressions Between the Logarithm of Squared Residual (LNE^2) and the Logarithm of the Suspected Proportionality Factor Z (LNZ)[1] (Standard Errors in Parentheses).

	Marxian Model		Durkheimian Model	
	Homicide $LN(E^2)$ b	Theft $LN(E^2)$ b	Homicide $LN(E^2)$ b	Theft $LN(E^2)$ b
Cross-Sectional Data				
LN(Z_6064)	.029 (.510)	-.003 (.423)	-.002 (.298)	-.041 (.191)
LN(Z_6569)	-.261 (.797)	-.830 (.081)	-.348 (.280)	.043 (.106)
LN(Z_7074)	-.473 .462	.332 (.812)	.106 (.349)	.404 (.510)
LN(Z_7579)	.206 (.528)	-.177 (.279)	.141 (.604)	.284 (.532)
LN(Z_8084)	1.450 (1.085)	1.087 (.631)	1.229 (1.449)	.355 (.316)
Pooled Data				
LN(Z_6074)	-.000 (.363)	-1.061* (.490)	.026 (.191)	.474 (.246)
LN(Z-7584)	.396 (.251)	.499* (.209)	.897* (.298)	.995* (.248)

[1] Residual E(s) are the saved residuals from baseline OLS regressions. The suspected proportionality factor Z(s) are the saved predicted probabilities of missing data from logistic regressions.
* $p < .05$.

Influential Cases: Cook's D, Studentized Residuals and Studentized Deleted Residuals

Table 12 provides a list of potential influential cases and outlier based on three types of residual analysis statistics. I include the top five high values (based on their absolute values) of residual indicators for each regression analysis. Criteria discussed in the previous chapter regarding the influential cases and outliers will be followed. In general, I will take the conservative approach that a nation is excluded only when it fails to meet at least two of the three criteria in a particular analysis.[6] The exclusion of cases is not permanent in the data set. Instead, it will be crime-specific (in analysis involving either homicide or theft), time-specific (in each of the five time periods) and model-specific (Durkheimian or Marxian). For each of the following regression analyses, we will provide a list of nations excluded for that particular analysis for being identified as outlier.

Multivariate Analyses

Cross-Sectional Data

Based on results from the preceding diagnostic tests for the cross-sectional data, I observed that (1) influential cases or outliers have been found in each of the baseline regression models across all five time periods; (2) only a few theoretical variables have significant effects on the likelihood of missing crime statistics; and (3) Park's test of heteroskedasticity does not give support to the use of Weighted Least Squares (WLS) estimation in cross-sectional analysis. Therefore, I apply the following strategies in my multivariate regression analyses using the cross-sectional data. First, I run Ordinary Least Squares (OLS) regression models excluding the identified influential cases. I provide a list of the nations that have been excluded in each of the particular regression analyses. Second, I add hazard rate instrumental variables into the relevant regression equations as corrections for the sample selection

Table 12:   Residual Analysis: Influential Cases and Outliers by Theoretical Perspective and Time Period.

	1960-1964	1965-1969	1970-1974	1975-1979	1980-1984
Marxian Perspective (Homicide)					
Cook's D					
	.609 (Korea)	.223 (Burma)	5.257 (Jamaica)	.486 (Israel)	.358 (Jamaica)
	.226 (N. Zealand)	.193 (Korea)	.309 (N. Zealand)	.228 (N. Zealand)	.326 (N. Zealand)
	.164 (Burma)	.098 (Denmark)	.095 (Korea)	.179 (Sweden)	.311 (Egypt)
	.087 (USA)	.080 (USA)	.071 (Zambia)	.151 (USA)	.302 (Kuwait)
	.060 (Denmark)	.056 (Italy)	.047 (Burma)	.110 (Philippines)	.128 (Cyprus)
Studentized Deleted Residuals					
	-3.950 (N. Zealand)	3.597 (Burma)	-3.344 (N. Zealand)	-1.920 (N. Zealand)	2.900 (Egypt)
	2.271 (Burma)	2.086 (USA)	-1.976 (Jamaica)	1.730 (USA)	2.159 (Kuwait)
	-2.112 (Korea)	1.893 (Italy)	1.942 (Burma)	-1.679 (Spain)	-1.542 (Cyprus)
	1.506 (Cyprus)	-1.714 (Brunei)	1.527 (Zambia)	1.572 (Sweden)	-1.503 (Norway)
	1.456 (Kuwait)	-1.492 (Korea)	-1.462 (Netherlands)	-1.325 (Norway)	-1.259 (N. Zealand)
Studentized Residuals					
	-3.345 (N. Zealand)	3.156 (Burma)	-2.934 (N. Zealand)	-1.784 (N. Zealand)	2.345 (Egypt)
	2.153 (Burma)	2.003 (USA)	-1.896 (Jamaica)	1.637 (USA)	1.922 (Kuwait)
	-2.020 (Korea)	1.834 (Italy)	1.867 (Burma)	-1.596 (Spain)	-1.471 (Cyprus)
	1.481 (Cyprus)	-1.674 (Brunei)	1.498 (Zambia)	1.508 (Sweden)	-1.440 (Norway)
	1.434 (Kuwait)	-1.470 (Korea)	-1.438 (Netherlands)	-1.297 (Norway)	-1.233 (N. Zealand)

Table 12 (cont.).

	1960-1964	1965-1969	1970-1974	1975-1979	1980-1984
			Marxian Perspective (Theft)		
Cook's D					
	.726 (Korea)	.668 (Jamaica)	3.877 (Jamaica)	1.178 (India)	2.080 (France)
	.445 (Philippines)	.186 (Kuwait)	.175 (Israel)	.245 (Israel)	.369 (Jamaica)
	.417 (Denmark)	.173 (Philippines)	.173 (Philippines)	.115 (Philippines)	.295 (Syria)
	.081 (USA)	.130 (Korea)	.054 (Kuwait)	.092 (Greece)	.176 (N. Zealand)
	.077 (Libya)	.088 (Denmark)	.040 (Monaco)	.087 (Finland)	.104 (Egypt)
Studentized Deleted Residuals					
	-4.049 (Philippines)	-3.548 (Philippines)	-4.305 (Philippines)	-3.594 (India)	-3.349 (Syria)
	2.350 (Korea)	-2.416 (Spain)	1.811 (Monaco)	2.287 (Israel)	2.327 (France)
	-2.282 (Spain)	-1.696 (Portugal)	1.741 (Israel)	-2.007 (Philippines)	2.162 (N. Zealand)
	1.954 (Denmark)	1.659 (Monaco)	1.490 (Scotland)	-1.671 (Portugal)	-1.819 (Egypt)
	1.361 (Monaco)	1.560 (Israel)	1.390 (Jamaica)	-1.318 (Syria)	-1.592 (Portugal)
Studentized Residuals					
	-3.428 (Philippines)	-3.133 (Philippines)	-3.460 (Philippines)	-2.976 (India)	-2.725 (Syria)
	2.225 (Korea)	-2.285 (Spain)	1.750 (Monaco)	2.121 (Israel)	2.106 (France)
	-2.168 (Spain)	-1.659 (Portugal)	1.688 (Israel)	-1.899 (Philippines)	1.987 (N. Zealand)
	1.887 (Denmark)	1.625 (Monaco)	1.463 (Scotland)	-1.617 (Portugal)	-1.722 (Egypt)
	1.346 (Monaco)	1.533 (Israel)	1.371 (Jamaica)	-1.299 (Syria)	-1.535 (Portugal)

Table 12 (cont.).

	1960-1964	1965-1969	1970-1974	1975-1979	1980-1984
			Durkheimian Perspective (Homicide)		
Cook's D					
	.177 (Netherlands)	.136 (UK)	.954 (Kuwait)	.592 (Kuwait)	.463 (Scotland)
	.165 (N. Zealand)	.117 (USA)	.160 (Luxembourg)	.220 (USA)	.304 (Jamaica)
	.100 (Libya)	.080 (Burma)	.132 (UK)	.156 (Philippines)	.175 (Egypt)
	.095 (Spain)	.070 (Libya)	.119 (N. Zealand)	.115 (Spain)	.076 (Canada)
	.059 (USA)	.069 (France)	.072 (Korea)	.080 (Singapore)	.048 (Cyprus)
Studentized Deleted Residuals					
	-3.751 (N. Zealand)	2.799 (Burma)	-3.216 (N. Zealand)	-2.285 (Spain)	2.830 (Jamaica)
	-1.962 (Netherlands)	2.143 (Italy)	2.004 (Burma)	1.502 (Italy)	-2.072 (Scotland)
	1.867 (Burma)	-1.953 (Brunei)	-1.845 (UK)	1.448 (Philippines)	-2.043 (Cyprus)
	-1.823 (Spain)	-1.839 (N. Zealand)	-1.807 (Netherland)	1.441 (Sweden)	1.776 (Egypt)
	1.719 (Cyprus)	1.717 (USA)	-1.693 (Brunei)	1.378 (Sri Lanka)	1.027 (Canada)
Studentized Residuals					
	-3.236 (N. Zealand)	2.591 (Burma)	-2.857 (N. Zealand)	-2.056 (Spain)	2.336 (Jamaica)
	-1.892 (Netherlands)	2.055 (Italy)	1.923 (Burma)	1.452 (Italy)	-1.876 (Scotland)
	1.809 (Burma)	-1.890 (Brunei)	-1.785 (UK)	1.406 (Philippines)	-1.856 (Cyprus)
	-1.770 (Spain)	-1.788 (N. Zealand)	-1.752 (Netherlands)	1.400 (Sweden)	1.661 (Egypt)
	1.676 (Cyprus)	1.678 (USA)	-1.650 (Brunei)	1.345 (Sri Lanka)	1.025 (Canada)

Table 12 (cont.).

	1960-1964	1965-1969	1970-1974	1975-1979	1980-1984
			Durkheimian Perspective (Theft)		
Cook's D					
	.159 (Philippines)	.675 (Kuwait)	1.640 (Kuwait)	5.852 (Kuwait)	.594 (Malawi)
	.111 (Spain)	.099 (Philippines)	.283 (Philippines)	.349 (Israel)	.382 (Portugal)
	.090 (Netherlands)	.093 (Portugal)	.080 (Germany)	.152 (Chile)	.251 (Syria)
	.075 (UK)	.083 (Kenya)	.071 (Israel)	.140 (Portugal)	.187 (Netherlands)
	.055 (France)	.068 (UK)	.050 (USA)	.095 (Singapore)	.095 (Scotland)
Studentized Deleted Residuals					
	-4.028 (Philippines)	-3.659 (Philippines)	-3.877 (Philippines)	-3.278 (Kuwait)	3.074 (Malawi)
	-1.991 (Spain)	1.962 (Kuwait)	1.781 (Monaco)	-2.243 (Greece)	-1.987 (Portugal)
	1.448 (Korea)	1.754 (Monaco)	-1.594 (Kuwait)	2.066 (Israel)	-1.888 (Syria)
	1.413 (Monaco)	-1.734 (Spain)	1.520 (Zambia)	-1.967 (India)	1.593 (Netherlands)
	-1.383 (France)	-1.460 (Portugal)	1.498 (Israel)	1.530 (Singapore)	-1.444 (Greece)
Studentized Residuals					
	-3.428 (Philippines)	-3.215 (Philippines)	-3.248 (Philippines)	-2.810 (Kuwait)	2.596 (Malawi)
	-1.921 (Spain)	1.899 (Kuwait)	1.726 (Monaco)	-2.092 (Greece)	-1.860 (Portugal)
	1.429 (Korea)	1.712 (Monaco)	-1.558 (Kuwait)	1.952 (Israel)	-1.782 (Syria)
	1.395 (Monaco)	-1.694 (Spain)	1.491 (Zambia)	-1.870 (India)	1.538 (Netherlands)
	-1.368 (France)	-1.441 (Portugal)	1.471 (Israel)	1.493 (Singapore)	-1.408 (Greece)

bias. I will discuss whether the sample selection bias has played a significant role in the regression analysis.

1) Test of Theoretical Models Using OLS Regression: Influential Cases Excluded

Table 13 displays the results of OLS estimation of the Marxian model on homicide for all five time periods in the cross-sectional data. Unemployment (UNEMP) had a significant positive effect on homicide in all but the 1975 to 1979 periods. Surplus value (SURPLUS) had a significant positive effect on homicide in the 1965-1969 period. Both observations are in the predicted direction which gives support to the Marxian perspective on homicide. Government expenditure (GOVEXP), semi-periphery nation status (SEMIPERI) and periphery nation status (PERIPH) had no significant effect on homicide in any of the five time periods. In addition, none of the Marxian explanatory variables were significant in the regression equation in the 1975-1979 period. The non-significant R square for the equation indicates a poor fit of the model specified based on the Marxian perspective for that particular time period.

Table 14 presents the results of OLS estimation of the Marxian model on theft for all five time periods in the cross-sectional data. Surplus value (SURPLUS) had a significant negative effect on theft in all but the 1970-1974 time periods. Unemployment (UNEMP), semi-periphery nation status (SEMIPERI) and periphery nation status (PERIPH) had no significant effect on theft in any of the five time periods. The R square for the Marxian perspective on theft for the 1960-1964 period was not significant. In addition, none of the Marxian perspective explanatory variables in the 1970-1974 model was statistically significant at the .05 level.

Table 15 and Table 16 include the results from the OLS estimations of the Durkheimian model for five cross-sectional time periods. Table 15 reveals that: (1) economic growth (GROWTH_1) had a significant negative effect on homicide in the 1980-1984 period; (2) industrialization (INDUS) had a significant negative effect on homicide in the 1965-1969 period; (3) urbanization (URBAN) had significant

Table 13: Homicide: OLS Estimation of the Marxian Model Using Cross-Sectional Data by Time Period (Standard Errors in Parentheses).

LNHOMIC

	1960-1964 b	1960-1964 β	1965-1969 b	1965-1969 β	1970-1974 b	1970-1974 β	1975-1979 b	1975-1979 β	1980-1984 b	1980-1984 β
UNEMP	.243* (.105)	.350*	.081* (.039)	.316*	.577* (.160)	.662*	.182 (.109)	.400	.110* (.030)	.783*
SURPLUS	.008 (.004)	.309	.005* (.002)	.539*	.000 (.002)	.039	.014 (.010)	.567	.010 (.009)	.330
GOVEXP	-.019 (.018)	-.149	.006 (.009)	.095	.019 (.016)	.215	.061 (.030)	.647	.040 (.021)	.457
SEMIPERI	.120 (.458)	.050	-.095 (.268)	-.065	-.097 (.413)	-.049	.198 (.569)	.096	-.699 (.483)	-.337
PERIPH	.131 (.458)	.054	-.365 (.311)	-.246	-.402 (.530)	-.184	.535 (.514)	.290	-.016 (.438)	-.008
INTERCEPT	-.035		.125		-1.438		-3.728		-2.357	
R²	.349*		.284*		.313*		.471		.673*	
Adj. R²	.253		.190		.202		.267		.537	
N	40		44		37		19		18	
Influential Nations	N. Zealand Burma Korea		Burma USA Italy		Jamaica N. Zealand Burma		N. Zealand		Egypt Kuwait	

* p < .05.

Table 14:   Theft: OLS Estimation of the Marxian Model Using Cross-Sectional Data by Time Period (Standard Errors in Parentheses).

LNTHEFT

	1960-1964 b	β	1965-1969 b	β	1970-1974 b	β	1975-1979 b	β	1980-1984 b	β
UNEMP	-.058 (.107)	-.092	-.034 (.133)	-.042	.025 (.225)	.023	-.008 (.075)	-.016	-.034 (.054)	-.131
SURPLUS	-.010* (.004)	-.467*	-.008* (.003)	-.441*	-.003 (.003)	-.186	-.026* (.006)	-.874*	-.043* (.014)	-.826*
GOVEXP	.004 (.024)	.028	-.028 (.026)	-.184	.013 (.023)	.119	-.014 (.019)	-.129	-.008 (.031)	-.051
SEMIPERI	.251 (.467)	.118	.088 (.463)	.038	-.872 (.509)	-.361	.125 (.508)	.039	-.033 (.687)	-.010
PERIPH	.024 (.442)	.012	-.495 (.523)	-.198	-1.037 (.623)	-.420	.034 (.495)	.013	-.273 (.761)	-.079
INTERCEPT	6.827*		8.123*		5.961*		10.081*		11.984*	
R^2	.230		.278*		.318*		.610*		.671*	
Adj. R^2	.120		.172		.196		.525		.575	
N	41		40		34		29		23	
Influential Nations	Philippines Korea Spain Denmark		Philippines Spain		Philippines Monaco Jamaica		India Israel Philippines		France Syria N. Zealand	

* $p < .05$.

positive effect on homicide in two time periods: 1960-1964 and 1970-1974; and (4) moral individualism (MORAL) had significant negative effect on homicide in two later time periods: 1975-1979 and 1980-1984. Democracy (DEMOC) had significant negative effect on homicide in 1960-1964 period. Both observations described in (1) and (2) are in the opposite directions as proposed. However, those described in (3) and (4) are in the predicted directions. The R square for the 1975-1979 equation was not significant which indicates a poor fit of model for that particular time period.

Table 16 reports the OLS estimations of the Durkheimian model on theft in five cross-sectional time periods. I found that: (1) economic growth (GROWTH_1) had a significant positive effect on theft in the 1960 to 1964 period; (2) neither industrialization (INDUS) nor urbanization (URBAN) had a significant effect on theft in any of the five cross-sectional time periods; and (3) moral individualism (MORAL) had a significant positive effect on theft in the two later time periods: 1975-1979 and 1980-1984. Democracy (DEMOC) had a significant positive effect on theft in the 1965 to 1969 period. Observations described in (1) are in the predicted directions. Those described in (3) are not.

2) *Brief Summary and Discussion*

Table 13 to table 16 provide the results of cross-sectional regression analyses testing both the Marxian and the Durkheimian perspectives. I excluded, conditionally, those detected influential cases before estimating each of these regressions. Nations listed under "influential nation" in each column are those excluded from the corresponding regression models. Notice that I have fewer nations included in each of the regression analyses at the later two time periods, 1975-1979 and 1980-1984. However, comparing the significant R square values across different time periods in each table, I find that the models seem to fit better in the later time periods, 1975-1979 and 1980-1984.

My findings thus far may be simply summarized. First, the hypothesized positive relationships between unemployment and homicide or between surplus value and homicide is indeed found. The effect of unemployment on homicide is

Table 15: Homicide: OLS Estimation of the Durkheimian Model Using Cross-Sectional Data by Time Period (Standard Errors in Parentheses).

LNHOMIC

	1960-1964 b	1960-1964 β	1965-1969 b	1965-1969 β	1970-1974 b	1970-1974 β	1975-1979 b	1975-1979 β	1980-1984 b	1980-1984 β
GROWTH_1	-.000	-.066	-.003	-.258	-.000	-.259	.000	.146	-.001*	-.669*
	(.002)		(.002)		(.000)		(.000)		(.000)	
INDUS	-.013	-.129	-.029*	-.442*	-.003	-.031	-.003	-.038	.002	.017
	(.020)		(.013)		(.019)		(.020)		(.022)	
URBAN	.014*	.379*	.004	.174	.021*	.537*	.008	.271	.003	.081
	(.007)		(.004)		(.007)		(.007)		(.007)	
MORAL	-	-	-	-	-	-	-.117*	-.525*	-.108*	-.454*
							(.051)		(.044)	
DEMOC	-.131*	-.525*	.003	.020	-.055	-.259	-	-	-	-
	(.044)		(.024)		(.037)					
INTERCEPT	1.929*		1.915*		1.391*		.715		.826	
R²	.283*		.274*		.313*		.311		.687*	
Adj. R²	.194		.191		.224		.115		.582	
N	37		40		36		22		17	
Influential Nations	N. Zealand Netherlands Burma Spain		Burma Italy Brunei N. Zealand		N. Zealand Burma UK Netherlands		Spain		Jamaica Scotland Cyprus	

* p < .05.

Table 16:   Theft: OLS Estimation of the Durkheimian Model Using Cross-Sectional Data by Time Period (Standard Errors in Parentheses)

	1960-1964 b	1960-1964 β	1965-1969 b	1965-1969 β	1970-1974 b	1970-1974 β	1975-1979 b	1975-1979 β	1980-1984 b	1980-1984 β
					LNTHEFT					
GROWTH_1	.005*	.366*	.004	.143	.000	.175	.001	.499	.000	.131
	(.002)		(.004)		(.000)		(.000)		(.000)	
INDUS	.037	.328	.015	.113	.024	.176	-.023	-.105	.070	.239
	(.020)		(.025)		(.029)		(.024)		(.008)	
URBAN	-.006	-.154	.000	.003	.004	.075	.003	.062	.004	.057
	(.007)		(.009)		(.010)		(.005)		(.008)	
MORAL	-	-	-	-	-	-	.182*	.490*	.426*	.731*
							(.050)		(.071)	
DEMOC	.017	.061	.110*	.357*	.074	.245	-	-	-	-
	(.044)		(.048)		(.058)					
INTERCEPT	4.344*		4.252*		4.422*		7.296*		7.094*	
R²	.313*		.238*		.258*		.776*		.784*	
Adj. R²	.237		.162		.163		.737		.739	
N	41		45		36		28		24	
Influential Nations	Philippines Spain		Philippines Kuwait		Philippines Monaco		Kuwait Greece Israel India		Malawi Portugal Syria	

* p < .05.

consistently statistically significant in four out of five cross-sectional time periods. It is not significant only in the 1975-1979 period. The effect of surplus value on homicide falls consistently in the predicted direction although it is significant in only one time period (1965-1969). Both unemployment and surplus value are among the most important predictors in the regression model based on the Marxian perspective. These findings give some support for the Marxian perspective on homicide.

Secondly, the predicted effects of urbanization and moral individualism on homicide are also observed. Urbanization has a significant positive effect on homicide in two time periods (1960-1964 and 1970-1974). Moral individualism or democracy has a negative effect on homicide in three time periods (1960-1964, 1975-1979, and 1980-1984). These observations are supportive of the Durkheimian perspective on homicide.

Third, I find that surplus value has a negative effect on theft in all but one cross-sectional time periods (not significant in the 1970-1974 period). It should be noted that this relationship is exactly the opposite of what was predicted by the Marxian perspective.

Fourth, I find a positive effect of economic growth on theft which is supportive of the Durkheimian perspective. Economic growth has a significant effect on theft in the 1960-1964 period. The direction of the relationship between economic growth and theft in other time periods is consistently positive (which is predicted) but not statistically significant.

Fifth, moral individualism or democracy was proposed to restrain criminal behavior in the Durkheimian perspective. I find, however, that it has positive effect on theft in three time periods, i.e., 1965-1969, 1975-1979 and 1980-1984. This observed positive relationship between moral individualism/democracy and theft was never predicted by my hypothesis.

From the above it is obvious that the tests of both the Marxian and the Durkheimian models using the cross-sectional data have yielded both predicted and unpredicted results. Given the small sample size, one should be skeptical about the regression results. I argue that further examination of the impact of possible sample selection bias is needed. To do so, I use the findings from previous diagnostic tests and rerun a total of eight regression models in which hazard rate instrument variables are added.

3)   Comparisons of Relevant OLS Regression Models With or Without Hazard Rate Instrumental Variables: Cross-Sectional Data

Table 17 to Table 19 report the OLS regression results from both the Marxian and the Durkheimian model after hazard rate instrument variables were added in selective substantive equations.[7] For the Marxian perspective, two regression models were rerun in which hazard rate variables are included. They are the Marxian perspective on homicide and theft in the 1975 to 1979 period. For the Durkheimian perspective, six regression models were re-estimated. These include the Durkheimian models on homicide and theft in each of the three time periods: 1970-1974, 1975-1979 and 1980-1984. Relevant findings reported in Table 13 to Table 16 are used to compare with those reported in Table 17 to Table 19.

Table 17 indicates that none of the corrected Marxian models for the 1975-1979 period are statistically significant.[8] Because the Marxian homicide model for the 1975-1979 period was not significant in the earlier analysis (see Table 13), I am not surprised to see that no significant change had occurred once the correction factor was added. Compared to the Marxian theft model for the same period (1975-1979) in table 14, the corrected model did not change the signs of any unstandardized regression coefficients. Surplus value continues to have a significant effect on theft. Nevertheless, the regression coefficient of the hazard rate variable is significant which implies effective sample selection bias. In addition, the corrected model is no longer statistically significant which indicates the deterioration of the model fit.

Table 18 shows that, in the corrected Durkheimian models on homicide for three time periods (1970-1974, 1975-1979 and 1980-1984), none of the regression coefficients for the hazard rate variables are statistically significant. This implies that sample selection does not pose a serious problem for these regression analyses. The

Table 17:   Homicide and Theft: OLS Estimation of the Marxian Model Using Cross-Sectional Data, Corrected for Sample Selection Bias (Standard Errors in Parentheses).

	LNHOMIC		LNTHEFT	
	1975-1979		1975-1979	
	b	β	b	β
UNEMP	.076	.174	-.004	-.008
	(.106)		(.068)	
SURPLUS	-.127	-.365	-.098*	-.522*
	(.148)		(.030)	
GOVEXP	.010	.140	-.010	-.090
	(.022)		(.018)	
SEMIPERI	.370	.187	.598	.187
	(.756)		(.496)	
PERIPH	.604	.304	.617	.229
	(.698)		(.504)	
HAZARD				
RATE	-6.917	-1.417	-7.500*	-1.114*
	(7.087)		(1.503)	
INTERCEPT	3.272		8.705*	
R^2	.279		.696	
Adj. R^2	.010		.613	
N	22		29	

* $p < .05$.

Table 18: Homicide: OLS Estimation of the Durkheimian Model Using Cross-Sectional Data, Corrected for Sample Selection Bias (Standard Errors in Parentheses).

| | LNHOMIC | | | | | |
| | 1970-1974 | | 1975-1979 | | 1980-1984 | |
	b	β	b	β	b	β
GROWTH_1	-.000	-.189	.000	.240	-.000*	-.616*
	(.000)		(.000)		(.000)	
INDUS	-.003	-.032	.012	.120	-.003	-.031
	(.019)		(.024)		(.023)	
URBAN	.020*	.532*	.006	.181	.003	.081
	(.007)		(.008)		(.008)	
MORAL	-	-	-1.710	-.405	.392	.123
	-		(2.599)		(.633)	
DEMOC	-.030	-.031	-	-	-	-
	(.167)		-		-	
HAZARD RATE	1.410	.251	2.640	.762	1.600	.394
	(.969)		(2.082)		(.873)	
INTERCEPT	.852		.059		.664	
	(.470)		(1.129)		(.797)	
R^2	.313*		.184		.703*	
Adj. R^2	.199		.071		.568	
N	36		22		17	

* $p < .05$.

effects of economic growth (GROWTH_1), industrialization (INDUS), and urbanization (URBAN) on homicide are comparable in both Table 15 and Table 18. The only exception is the effect of moral individualism (MORAL) on homicide in the 1975-1979 and the 1980-1984 periods. For example, moral individualism (MORAL) had significant negative effects on homicide in both the 1975-1979 and the 1980-1984 period in Table 15. But, the effects of moral individualism (MORAL) on homicide become positive when the hazard rate variable is added in the same regression equations and they are no longer significant. Overall, the R square values of the corresponding regression models in both Table 15 and Table 18 are very close.

Table 19 reports the results of the corrected Durkheimian model on theft. I find that the hazard rate was significant in each of the two later time periods: 1975-1979 and 1980-1984. The negative sign of the regression coefficient for the hazard rate variable suggests that nations for which the probability of missing crime statistics are higher are those with a lower theft rate. Therefore, it is possible that the sample nations selected in the equation might have under-represented those nations with lower theft rates. In spite of the detected sample selection bias, the regression coefficients, the intercepts and R squares in the corrected time-specific Durkheimian models on theft (reported in Table 19) changed little compared to those without correction factors (reported in Table 16). This leads to the following discussion of the utility of the correction procedure in dealing with sample selection bias.

4) Discussion and Conclusion: To Treat or Not to Treat

As discussed previously, Berk (1983) strongly recommended that sample selection bias be suspected until proven absent and correction for censored sampling effects should be a routine practice. I applied Berk's (1983) suggestion in my study. I ran diagnostic tests first to determine whether sample selection bias exists. I found that sample selection bias did exist in some analyses involving some time periods but not others. Thus, I applied the correction procedure selectively based on the diagnosis.

Table 19:   Theft: OLS Estimation of the Durkheimian Model Using Cross-Sectional
Data, Corrected for Sample Selection Bias (Standard Errors in Parentheses).

	LNTHEFT					
	1970-1974		1975-1979		1980-1984	
	b	β	b	β	b	β
GROWTH_1	.000	.124	.001*	.449*	.000	.075
	(.000)		(.000)		(.002)	
INDUS	.022	.163	-.021	-.094	.069	.236
	(.029)		(.024)		(.037)	
URBAN	.003	.053	.004	.077	.004	.057
	(.010)		(.006)		(.009)	
MORAL	-	-	.559	.166	.417*	.597*
	-		(.391)		(.168)	
DEMOC	.363	.171	-	-	-	-
	(.383)		-		-	
HAZARD						
RATE	-2.198	-.236	-2.918*	-.461*	-5.612*	-.662*
	(1.723)		(.823)		(1.067)	
INTERCEPT	5.446*		7.117*		7.123*	
	(.770)		(.682)		(.977)	
R^2	.272*		.785*		.785*	
Adj. R^2	.151		.736		.726	
N	36		28		24	

* $p < .05$.

I compared the results from regression models with and without the correction factor-hazard rate instrumental variable included in the equation. Observable changes (in the intercepts and the unstandardized regression coefficients) did occur but they did not overwhelmingly alter the interpretation of the theoretical model. In only one circumstance, i.e., Marxian model on theft in the 1975-1979 period, the corrected regression model was no longer significant compared to the previous one without correction. In general, even when hazard rate instrumental variables were found to have significant effects on the dependent variables (in the Marxian model on theft, 1975-1979, Durkheimian theft model in 1975-1979 and in 1980-1984), the directions and the significant effects of the explanatory variables in relevant equations did not change significantly.

I realize that the consequences of the selection bias correction procedure in this study may have been influenced by my small sample size. In fact, past research has shown that "in small , severely censored samples, even if normality assumptions are true, unless one has a strong enough theory to justify the assumption that selection errors and regression errors are very highly correlated, it is exceedingly difficult to know whether Heckman's estimator worsens or cures censoring bias" (Stolzenberg and Relles, 1990:408). Other researchers argue that maximum likelihood methods are more efficient compared to the Heckman's procedure exemplified in Berk's (1982, 1983) studies (Nelson, 1984; Paarsch, 1984; Little and Rubin, 1987).

I suggest that it is necessary to take into consideration the sample selection issue in any quantitative comparative cross-national study. Whether or not to treat selection bias has to depend on both theory and the statistical diagnosis. In any case, sample size should be a primary concern before one incorporates the sample correction procedure into substantive discussion of the results. If the sample is relatively small, one may run the risk of not being able to determine the true impact of any treatment of the selection bias. Due to the small sample size in my cross-sectional data, I will only use the corrected models as a supplement to the analyses done on the pooled data, not as the basis on which conclusions are drawn.

Pooled Data

Starting from this section, I will present multivariate regression results using the pooled data. The following presentation of the results from the pooled analysis is divided into five major parts. First, I will present the test results for each of the theoretical perspectives separately. I run regressions using the total sample as well as using the sub-samples (e.g., developed vs. developing nations for the Durkheimian perspective, or non-core nations vs. core nations for the Marxian perspective). I provide comparisons between them in two pooled time periods. Second, I run Weighted Least Squares (WLS) regression to treat the heteroskedasticity problems in models identified by the previous diagnostic tests. Results from OLS and WLS for the respective models are compared. Third, I run Least Squares Dummy Variable models (LSDV) for each of the two theoretical perspectives using nation dummies in the equation. Fourth, I construct nested models in which each theoretical perspective serves as control for the other. A common set of other control variables as well as the theoretically relevant interaction terms are also included.

1) Separate OLS Estimations of the Theoretical Models Using Pooled Data

Tables 20 and 21 provides the test results of the Durkheimian perspective on crime in each of the two pooled time periods. Model 1 is the regression analysis using the entire sample including all the available nations. Model 2 uses only the developed nation sub-sample. Model 3 uses only the developing nation sub-sample. A few comparisons can be made using these two tables. First, comparisons can be made between Model 1, Model 2 and Model 3. Second, Model 1, Model 2 and Model 3 in each time period can be compared to the corresponding ones in the other time period.

Table 20: OLS Estimation of the Durkheimian Model on Homicide Using the Pooled Data by Time Period (Standard Errors in Parentheses).

LNHOMIC

	1960-1974						1975-1984					
	Model 1		Model 2		Model 3		Model 1		Model 2		Model 3	
	All Nations		Developed		Developing		All Nations		Developed		Developing	
	b	β	b	β	b	β	b	β	b	β	b	β
GROWTH_1	-.000	-.061	.000	.012	-.000	-.057	-.000	-.118	-.000	-.079	-.000	-.199
	(.000)		(.000)		(.000)		(.000)		(.000)		(.000)	
URBAN	.003*	.093*	.006*	.211*	.000	.029	.002	.053	.002	.093	.028*	.609*
	(.001)		(.002)		(.002)		(.002)		(.002)		(.007)	
INDUS	-1.051	-.095	.017*	.142*	.002	.014	-.717	-.077	.032*	.338*	-.024*	-.270*
	(.560)		(.008)		(.009)		(.668)		(.008)		(.011)	
MORAL	-	-	-	-	-	-	-.067*	-.304*	.078*	.227*	-.117*	-.410*
	-		-		-		(.016)		(.030)		(.044)	
DEMOC	-.047*	-.223*	-.017*	.142*	-.020	-.099	-	-	-	-	-	-
	(.010)		(.008)		(.013)		-		-		-	
INTERCEPT	1.923*		.612*		1.774*		2.530*		-.271		3.094*	
R²	.065*		.074*		.012		.135*		.163*		.304*	
Adj. R²	.058		.057		.003		.117		.139		.250	
N	501		225		276		198		142		56	

* p<.05.

1960-1974 Time Period

Table 20 reveals that in the 1960-1974 period (1) democracy (DEMOC) had a significant negative effect on homicide in both Model 1 and Model 2; (2) urbanization (URBAN) had a significant positive effect on homicide in both Model 1 and Model 2; and (3) industrialization (INDUS) had a significant positive effect on homicide in Model 2. All of these observations are supportive to the hypotheses derived from the Durkheimian perspective. Nevertheless, none of the explanatory variables in Model 3 had a significant effect on homicide in the 1960-1974 period. The R square is also not significant at the .05 level in Model 3. This indicates that in the 1960-1974 period, the Durkheimian model on homicide does not fit well for the developing nation sub-sample.

1975-1984 Time Period

Table 20 also shows that in the 1975-1984 period (1) moral individualism (MORAL) had a significant negative effect on homicide in Model 1; (2) in Model 2, industrialization (INDUS) had a significant positive effect on homicide. But, the effect of moral individualism on homicide is positive which is not predicted; (3) in Model 3, urbanization (URBAN) had a significant positive effect on homicide. Moral individualism had a significant negative effect on homicide. Both are in the predicted directions. Industrialization (INDUS) had a significant negative effect on homicide in Models 2 and 3 which is not predicted.

Table 21 reports the regression results from the Durkheimian perspective on theft. Economic growth (GROWTH_1) had a positive effect on theft in Model 1 in both time periods. Industrialization (INDUS) had a significant positive effect on theft in both Model 1 and Model 2 in the 1960-1974 time period but only in Model 1 in the 1975-1984 period. All these observations are in the predicted direction. The effects of moral individualism (MORAL) and democracy (DEMOC) on theft, however, were consistently in the unpredicted directions. Both had a significant positive effect on theft in both time periods. And, the direction of these effects do not seem to change in different models.

Table 21: OLS Estimation of the Durkheimian Model on Theft Using the Pooled Data by Time Period (Standard Errors in Parentheses).

LNTHEFT

	1960-1974						1975-1984					
	Model 1		Model 2		Model 3		Model 1		Model 2		Model 3	
	All Nations		Developed		Developing		All Nations		Developed		Developing	
	b	β	b	β	b	β	b	β	b	β	b	β
GROWTH_1	.000*	.084*	.000	.072	.000	.062	.000*	.096*	.000	.114	.000	.085
	(.000)		(.000)		(.000)		(.000)		(.000)		(.000)	
URBAN	.003	.056	.004	.082	-.006	-.075	-.000	-.000	-.002	-.061	.006	.106
	(.003)		(.003)		(.005)		(.003)		(.003)		(.005)	
INDUS	2.582*	.135*	.029*	.140*	.008	.029	2.693*	.116*	.004	.020	.023	.121
	(.911)		(.012)		(.016)		(1.014)		(.014)		(.017)	
MORAL	-	-	-	-	-	-	.300*	.663*	.374*	.498*	.199*	.445*
							(.020)		(.051)		(.039)	
DEMOC	.108*	.301*	.229*	.510*	.038	.106	-	-	-	-	-	-
	(.017)		(.026)		(.023)							
INTERCEPT	4.048*		2.931*		4.763*		3.016*		2.806*		3.565*	
R^2	.174*		.348*		.017		.527*		.297*		.218*	
Adj. R^2	.167		.336		.003		.520		.279		.188	
N	499		221		278		280		169		111	

* $p<.05$.

Table 22 and Table 23 are the regression results of the Marxian perspective on crime tested in each of the two pooled time periods. Table 22 shows that unemployment (UNEMP) and surplus value (SURPLUS) had significant positive effects on homicide in different models as well as in different time periods. The only exception is in Model 3 in the 1960-1974 period. Semi-periphery nation status (SEMIPERI) and Periphery nation status (PERIPH) had no significant effect on homicide in the early time period (1960-1974) but both had significant positive effects on homicide in the later time period (1975-1984). The effect of government expenditure (GOVEXP) on homicide was not significant in model 1 in the 1960-1974 period. In the 1975-1984 period, government expenditure had a significant effect on homicide in all models. The effect of government expenditure on homicide is positive in both Model 1 and Model 2 but it is negative in Model 3.

Table 23 displays the results of the Marxian model on theft for each of the two pooled time periods. I found that unemployment (UNEMP) and surplus value (SURPLUS) had quite consistent negative effects on theft in both time periods. The only exception was in the 1975-1984 period in which unemployment had a significant positive effect on theft using the Core nation sample (Model 2). Government expenditure (GOVEXP) had a positive effect on theft in Model 1 in the 1960-1974 period. Government expenditure had a significant positive effect on theft in Model 2 (Core nation sample) in both time periods. Semi-periphery nation status (SEMIPERI) and Periphery nation status (PERIPH) both had significant negative effects on theft in Model 1 in the 1975-1984 period. Both had no significant effect on theft in the 1960-1974 period.

2) Weighted Least Square Estimations of the Theoretical Perspectives Using Pooled Data

My earlier diagnostic test (see Table 11) indicates that on four occasions the suspected proportionality factor Z, i.e., the probability of missing crime statistics had significant impact on the variance of the error term. This violates the regression assumption that variance of the error term should be a constant. Thus, I reestimated

Table 22: Homicide: OLS Estimation of the Marxian Model Using the Pooled Data by Time Period (Standard Errors in Parentheses).

LNHOMIC

	1960-1974						1975-1984					
	Model 1		Model 2		Model 3		Model 1		Model 2		Model 3	
	All Nations		Core		Non-Core		All Nations		Core		Non-Core	
	b	β	b	β	b	β	b	β	b	β	b	β
UNEMP	.073*	.173	.178*	.391*	-.004*	-.009	.058*	.354	.050*	.272*	.085*	.571*
	(.021)		(.031)		(.026)		(.011)		(.016)		(.015)	
SURPLUS	.002*	.154*	.002	.066	.003*	.188	.001	.061	-.000	-.038	.011*	.287*
	(.000)		(.002)		(.000)		(.002)		(.002)		(.004)	
SEMIPERI	.169	.098	-	-	-	-	.440*	.244*	-	-	-	-
	(.096)						(.144)					
PERIPH	.059	.033	-	-	-	-	.497*	.290*	-	-	-	-
	(.107)						(.127)					
GOVEXP	.002	.201	-.006	-.067	.008	.089	.016*	.232*	.022*	.414*	-.028*	-.222*
	(.004)		(.006)		(.005)		(.006)		(.006)		(.012)	
INTERCEPT	.670*		.656*		.866*		.310		.279		1.101	
R²	.092		.172*		.033*		.238*		.211*		.307*	
Adj. R²	.083		.159		.023		.219		.182		.279	
N	501		190		311		198		119		79	

* p<.05.

Table 23: Theft: OLS Estimation of the Marxian Model Using the Pooled Data by Time Period (Standard Errors in Parentheses).

LNTHEFT

| | 1960–1974 | | | | | | 1975–1984 | | | | | |
| | Model 1 All Nations | | Model 2 Core | | Model 3 Non-Core | | Model 1 All Nations | | Model 2 Core | | Model 3 Non-Core | |
	b	β	b	β	b	β	b	β	b	β	b	β
UNEMP	-.168* (.035)	-.230*	-.186* (.054)	-.221*	-.129* (.043)	-.167*	.017 (.019)	.044	.088* (.025)	.242*	-.017 (.027)	-.050
SURPLUS	-.004* (.001)	-.174*	-.016* (.003)	-.324*	-.004* (.001)	-.160*	-.016* (.002)	-.408*	-.015* (.002)	-.504*	-.017* (.004)	-.365*
SEMIPERI	-.081 (.155)	-.028	-	-	-	-	-.815* (.192)	-.008*	-	-	-	-
PERIPH	-.150 (.175)	-.048	-	-	-	-	-.997* (.188)	-.284*	-	-	-	-
GOVEXP	.014* (.007)	.092*	.044* (.010)	.289*	-.009 (.009)	-.059	.013 (.007)	.092	.026* (.009)	.227*	.009 (.011)	.064
INTERCEPT	6.175*		6.164*		6.710*		8.135*		7.015*		7.762*	
R²	.145*		.308*		.052*		.419*		.425*		.148*	
Adj. R²	.136		.297		.043		.409		.412		.129	
N	499		185		314		280		140		140	

* p<.05.

the following regression models using the weighted least squares (WLS) technique: (1) Marxian models on theft for both of the two pooled time periods, 1960-1974 and 1975-1984; and (2) Durkheimian models on both homicide and theft for the later pooled time period, i.e., 1975-1984. The results are reported in Table 24.

Table 24 reveals that, first of all, for the Marxian perspective on theft in both time periods--1960-1974 and 1975-1984--the results from Model 1 in Table 23 (OLS estimation) and those from Table 24 (WLS estimation) are almost identical.[9] Second, for the Durkheimian perspective on homicide in the 1975-1984 period, the results from Model 1 in Table 20 and from the corresponding model in Table 24 both show that moral individualism (MORAL) is the only variable which has a significant negative effect on homicide. The unstandardized coefficients and intercepts are also comparable. Third, for the Durkheimian perspective on theft in the 1975-1984 period, the results from Model 1 in Table 21 and those from the corresponding model in Table 24 also indicate their comparability. Economic growth (GROWTH_1) and moral individualism (MORAL) both had significant positive effects on theft regardless of the estimation methods. It is worth noticing that industrialization (INDUS) which had a significant positive effect on theft in the OLS estimation is no longer significant in the WLS estimation.

Based on the above observations, I conclude that using Weighted Least Squares (WLS) estimations to remedy heteroskedasticity problem does not produce results that are substantially different from the ordinary least squares (OLS) estimations. The OLS estimators appear to be quite robust. The standard errors from the OLS estimation are not necessarily less efficient than those from the WLS estimation. The overall model fit statistics also indicate that the impact of choosing between OLS and WLS methods is not great. In fact, I observed greater R square values generated by OLS estimations compared to those generated by the WLS estimations in the current study.

Table 24: Homicide and Theft: Weighted Least Square (WLS) Estimations of the Durkheimian and the Marxian Models Using Pooled Data by Time Period (Standard Errors in Parentheses).

	Marxian Perspective Theft		Durkheimian Perspective	
	1960-1974	1975-1984	Homicide 1975-1984	Theft 1975-1984
UNEMP	-.162* -.231*	.034 .080	- -	- -
	(.033)	(.020)		
SURPLUS	-.003* -.153*	-.020* -.463*	- -	- -
	(.001)	(.002)		
SEMIPERI	-.093 -.032	-.800* -.182*	- -	- -
	(.158)	(.218)		
PERIPH	-.141 -.049	-.737* -.188*	- -	- -
	(.170)	(.199)		
GOVEXP	.008 .051	.014* .103*	- -	- -
	(.007)	(.007)		
URBAN	- -	- -	.000 .005	-.001 -.026
			(.002)	(.002)
MORAL	- -	- -	-.078* -.314*	.341* .664*
			(.018)	(.023)
INDUS	- -	- -	.573 .063	.956 .044
			(.653)	(.950)
GROWTH_1	- -	- -	-.000 -.085	.000 .146*
			(.000)	(.000)
INTERCEPT	6.269*	8.370*	2.390*	2.968*
R^2	.119*	.451*	.104*	.511*
Adj. R^2	.110	.441	.085	.503
N	499	280	198	280

* $p < .05$.

3) Least Square Dummy Variable (LSDV) Estimations of Both the Durkheimian and the Marxian Models with Nation Dummy Variables Included

Table 25 reports the results from LSDV estimations of the Durkheimian model on both homicide and theft in two time periods. I created dummy variables representing each of the developed nations in the sample. The developing nations, as a whole, serve as the reference group. Regression analyses were run including all the Durkheimian explanatory variables and all the developed nation dummy variables.

The results reported in Table 25 show that first, democracy (DEMOC) had a significant negative effect on homicide in the 1960-1974 period after the nation specific effects are controlled in the analysis. The majority of the developed nation dummy variables had significant negative effects on homicide in the 1960-1974 period. The exceptions are: France, Italy, and United States which had a significant positive effect on homicide. Second, in the second time period (1975-1984), urbanization (URBAN) had a significant positive effect on homicide after controlling for the nation-specific effects from the developed nations. Similar to the observation from the first time period, all significant nation-specific effects on homicide are negative. This indicates that the characteristics of these developed nations have consistently kept their homicide rates lower than the average of the reference group (i.e., the intercept) in both of the two pooled time period.[10]

A different picture is notable in Table 25 for the Durkheimian model on theft. Both moral individualism (MORAL) and democracy (DEMOC) had a significant positive effect on theft in each of the two time periods. The coefficients for the nation dummy variables reveal that the majority of the developed nations had a significant positive effect on theft in both time periods. Portugal, Spain and Greece are the only exceptions. The dummy variables for Portugal and Spain had significant negative effect on theft in the 1960-1974 period. The dummy variables for Portugal and Greece have significant negative effects on theft in the 1975-1984 period.

Table 25: Homicide and Theft: LSDV Estimation of the Durkheimian Model Using Pooled Data and Including Developed Nation Dummy Variables by Time Period (Standard Errors in Parentheses).

	LNHOMIC				LNTHEFT			
	1960-1974		1975-1984		1960-1974		1975-1984	
	b	β	b	β	b	β	b	β
GROWTH_1	-.000	-.019	-.000	-.089	.000	.032	.000	.028
	(.000)		(.000)		(.000)		(.000)	
URBAN	.000	.023	.008*	.268*	-.003	-.064	.005	.083
	(.001)		(.003)		(.003)		(.003)	
INDUS	.344	.031	-1.291	-.139	.656	.034	1.550	.067
	(.519)		(.699)		(.909)		(1.100)	
MORAL	-		-.026	-.118	-		.195*	.431*
	-		(.025)		-		(.026)	
DEMOC	-.019*	-.090*	-		.034*	.096*	-	
	(.009)		-		(.017)		-	
INTERCEPT	1.732*		2.121*		4.798*		6.703*	
AUSTRALIA	-.305		-.479*		-.308		.177	
AUSTRIA	-.931*		-.379		1.263*		.657	
CANADA	-.589*		-.718*		-.625		1.545*	
DENMARK	-1.024*		-.329		2.161*		1.567*	
FINLAND	-.534*		-		.387		1.187*	
FRANCE	.462*		-		-.389		.185	
GERMANY	-1.048*		.127		2.432*		1.505*	
GREECE	-		-.961*		-.451		-1.179*	
ITALY	.976*		.205		1.023*		.107	
JAPAN	-.419*		-1.040*		1.118*		.077	
LUXEMBOURG	.194		-		1.195*		-	
NETHERLAND	-1.334*		-		-.408		1.302*	
N. ZEALAND	-1.568*		-.949*		.061		1.555*	
NORWAY	-1.251*		-1.189*		-.348		1.034*	
PORTUGAL	-.371*		-.694*		-1.355*		-1.267*	
SCOTLAND	-.907*		-1.244*		1.977*		.520	
SPAIN	-1.388*		-1.384*		-2.180*		.633	
SWEDEN	-.548*		.362		1.689*		2.057*	
UK	-1.169*		-.685*		2.284*		1.565*	
USA	.835*		.205		2.303*		1.403*	
R^2	.502*		.606*		.490*		.728*	
Adj. R^2	.478		.562		.464		.703	
N	501		198		499		280	

* $p < .05$.

Table 26 reports the estimations of the Durkheimian model by adding developing nation dummy variables into regression equations. Developed nations serve as the reference group. I found that in the 1960-1974 period (1) both urbanization (URBAN) and industrialization (INDUS) had significant positive effects on homicide; (2) the majority of the developing nation dummy variables had significant positive effects on homicide. Brunei was the only nation that had a significant negative effect on homicide in that time period. In the 1975-1984 period, economic growth (GROWTH_1) had a significant negative effect on homicide. Both industrialization and moral individualism had significant positive effect on homicide. Estimations for some nation dummy variables were not possible because of missing data in the dependent variable. Almost all the available developing nation dummy variables had significant positive effects on homicide.

In Table 26, the estimations from the Durkheimian theft model in the 1960-1974 period reveal that: (1) urbanization (URBAN), industrialization (INDUS) and democracy all had significant positive effects on theft; and (2) four developing nation dummy variables had significant negative effects on theft. They are India, Peru, Philippines, Sri Lanka and Turkey. For the 1975-1984 time period, both economic growth (GROWTH_1) and moral individualism had significant effect on theft. Only the following nation dummy variables had a significant positive effect on theft: Chile, Israel, Malawi, Singapore and Zambia.

Table 27 displays the estimation results form LSDV regression models based on the Marxian perspective on crime. Dummy variables for the core nations are constructed while the non-core (i.e., semi-periphery and periphery) nations serve as the reference group.

In the Marxian homicide model, I observed that: (1) the predicted positive effects of surplus value (SURPLUS) on homicide were found in each of the two pooled time periods; (2) unemployment had a significant positive effect on homicide only in the 1975-1984 period; (3) government expenditure did not show any significant effect on homicide; and (4) the nation dummy variables for France, Italy,

Table 26:   Homicide and Theft: LSDV Estimation of the Durkheimian Model Using Pooled Data and Including Developing Nation Dummy Variables by Time Period (Standard Errors in Parentheses).

	LNHOMIC				LNTHEFT			
	1960-1974		1975-1984		1960-1974		1975-1984	
	b	β	b	β	b	β	b	β
GROWTH_1	-.000	-.032	-.000*	-.095	.000	.044	.000*	.065
	(.000)		(.000)		(.000)		(.000)	
URBAN	.004*	.146	.002	.068	.004*	.086	-.003	-.057
	(.001)		(.002)		(.002)		(.002)	
INDUS	1.360*	.123	3.130*	.338	2.435*	.127	.670	.029
	(.512)		(.682)		(.744)		(1.192)	
MORAL	-	-	.073*	.330	-	-	.305*	.674
	-	-	(.026)		-	-	(.040)	
DEMOC	-.009	-.043	-	-	.187*	.520	-	-
	(.012)		-	-	(.017)		-	-
INTERCEPT	.695*		.919*		3.471*		8.196*	
BRUNEI	-.646*		-		.093		-	
BURMA	2.643*		-		.281		-	
CHILE	.823*		-		-.354		1.236*	
CYPRUS	1.294*		-.757		.133		-1.132*	
EGYPT	.819*		2.190*		1.295*		-1.649*	
FIJI	.155		.454*		-.578		-.257	
HONGKONG	-.103		-		.594*		-	
INDIA	.346		-		-1.532*		-2.070*	
INDONESIA	.037		-		1.547*		-.970*	
ISRAEL	-.157		1.327*		1.539*		1.415*	
IVORY C.	.493		-		1.345*		-	
JAMAICA	.906*		2.026*		-.068		-.526	
KENYA	.999*		-		-.196		-	
KOREA	-.011		-		1.370*		-.077	
KUWAIT	1.296*		2.293*		1.918*		-.257	
LEBANON	1.115*		-		.347		-	
LIBYA	1.404*		-		1.058*		-	
MALAWI	.564*		-		1.308*		2.067*	
MALAYSIA	.518*		-		.216		-.699	
MONACO	-		-		2.196*		-	
MOROCCO	.000		-		.652		-.964	
NIGERIA	.052		-		-.361		-	
PERU	1.086*		-		-1.196*		-	
PHILIPPINE	1.183*		1.788*		-4.032*		-1.600*	

Table 26 (cont.)

	LNHOMIC		LNTHEFT	
	1960-1974 b β	1975-1984 b β	1960-1974 b β	1975-1984 b β
SINGAPORE	.349*	.245*	1.296*	1.106*
SRILANKA	1.275*	1.221*	-.662*	-.954*
SYRIA	1.455*	1.390*	-.305	-1.419*
TURKEY	1.254*	-	-1.710*	-
ZAMBIA	1.204*	1.553*	1.888*	1.033*
R^2	.521	.611	.658	.743
Adj. R^2	.488	.579	.633	.721
N	501	198	499	280

* $p<.05$.

Table 27:   Homicide and Theft: LSDV Estimation of the Marxian Model Using Pooled Data and Including Core Nation Dummy Variables by Time Period (Standard Errors in Parentheses).

VARIABLE	LNHOMIC				LNTHEFT			
	1960-1974		1975-1984		1960-1974		1975-1984	
	b	β	b	β	b	β	b	β
SURPLUS	.003*	.167*	.008*	.332*	-.003*	-.134*	-.012*	-.309*
	(.000)		(.003)		(.001)		(.002)	
UNEMP	-.013	-.032	.065*	.392*	-.131*	-.180*	.007	.017
	(.020)		(.010)		(.033)		(.019)	
GOVEXP	.008	.089	-.015	-.222	-.003	-.020	.009	.064
	(.004)		(.008)		(.006)		(.008)	
INTERCEPT	.926*		1.209*		6.454*		6.972*	
AUSTRALIA	-.102		-.008		-.759*		.365	
AUSTRIA	-.805*		.386*		.957*		1.094*	
CANADA	-.356*		-.408*		-.834*		1.825*	
DENMARK	-1.053*		-.105		1.963*		1.785*	
FRANCE	.715*		-		-.613*		1.341*	
GERMANY	-.868*		.614*		1.757*		1.662*	
GREECE	-		-1.237*		-.444		-.088	
ITALY	1.059*		.729*		.749*		.259	
JAPAN	-.348		-.239		.572		.509	
LUXEMBOURG	.421*		-		.992*		-	
NETHERLANDS	-1.133*		-		-1.215*		1.664*	
NORWAY	-1.105*		-.309		-.828*		1.275*	
PORTUGAL	.003		.102		-1.688*		-.768	
SPAIN	-1.064*		-.794*		-2.607*		.015	
SWEDEN	-.397		1.397*		1.077*		1.879*	
UK	-.870*		-.364		1.510*		1.729*	
USA	1.184*		.964*		1.916*		1.895*	
R^2	.388		.511		.459		.548	
Adj. R^2	.364		.464		.437		.515	
N	501		198		499		280	

* $p<.05$.

Luxembourg and United States had significant positive effects on homicide in the 1960-1974 period. In the 1975-1984 period, the nation dummy variables for Austria, Germany, Italy, Sweden and United States had significant positive effects on homicide.

In the Marxian theft model, I found that, first, both surplus value (SURPLUS) and unemployment (UNEMP) had significant negative effects on theft. These findings were not predicted in the hypotheses. Second, in the 1960-1974 period, no clear pattern of either positive or negative effects of core nation dummies on theft can be found. The nation dummy variables for Australia, Canada, France, Netherlands, Norway, Portugal and Spain had significant negative effect on theft. Those nation dummy variables representing Austria, Denmark, Germany, Italy, Luxembourg, Sweden, UK, and USA had significant positive effects on theft. However, in the 1975-1984 period, it is more clearly shown that the majority of the core nation dummies have significant positive effect on theft.

Table 28 reports the LSDV estimations of the Marxian model including the non-core nation dummy variables. I construct a nation dummy variable for each of the semi-periphery and periphery nations, using the core nation as the reference group. First, I found that unemployment had a significant positive effect on homicide in both time periods. Second, in the 1960-1974 period, some of the non-core nation dummies such as those for Brunei, Hong Kong, Israel, Korea, New Zealand, Nigeria and Scotland had a significant negative effect on homicide. However, most of the non-core nation dummy variables had positive effect on homicide. Third, in the 1975-1984 period, unemployment and surplus value both had significant positive effect on homicide. Most of the available non-core nation dummy variables had a significant positive effects on homicide. The nation dummy variable for New Zealand is the exception which had a significant negative effect on homicide. Missing data problem in homicide is acute for the analysis involving the 1975-1984 period.

Table 28:   Homicide and Theft: LSDV Estimation of the Marxian Model Using Pooled Data and Including Semiperiphery and Periphery Nation Dummy Variables by Time Period (Standard Errors in Parentheses).

VARIABLE	LNHOMIC				LNTHEFT			
	1960-1974		1975-1984		1960-1974		1975-1984	
	b	β	b	β	b	β	b	β
SURPLUS	-.001	-.077	-.000	-.012	-.004*	-.152*	-.014*	-.363*
	(.000)		(.002)		(.001)		(.002)	
UNEMP	.110*	.262*	.050*	.301*	-.135*	-.185*	.080*	.199*
	(.000)		(.014)		(.027)		(.020)	
GOVEXP	-.005	-.051	.023*	.330*	.034*	.219*	.025*	.177*
	(.003)		(.005)		(.006)		(.007)	
INTERCEPT	1.184*		.178		5.164*		7.076*	
BRUNEI	-1.058*		-		-.212*		-	
BURMA	2.444*		-		-.552*		-	
CHILE	.674*		-		-.697		-1.120*	
CYPRUS	.954*		-.748		-.128		-.964*	
EGYPT	.408		1.547*		-.573		-3.020*	
FIJI	-.352		.163		-.296		-.052	
FINLAND	.109		-		-.803*		-	
HONGKONG	-.557*		-		.196		-	
INDIA	-.025		-		-1.004*		-2.800*	
INDONESIA	-.404		-		.055		-2.480*	
IVORY C.	.042		-		-.086		-	
ISRAEL	-.674*		1.302*		1.927*		2.001*	
JAMAICA	.171		.821*		.601		-2.840*	
KENYA	.528*		-		-1.068*		-	
KOREA	-.437*		-		1.572*		.410	
KUWAIT	.898*		1.563*		.785*		-.928*	
LEBANON	.627*		-		-.309		-	
LIBYA	.983*		-		.082		-	
MALAYSIA	.080		-		.141		-1.160*	
MALAWI	.185		-		.064		-	
MONACO	-		-		1.860		-	
MOROCCO	-.400		-		-.632		-	
NEWZEALAND	-1.350*		-.340*		-.381		.978*	
NIGERIA	-.492*		-		-1.230*		-	
PERU	.896*		-		-1.202*		-	
PHILIPPINE	.535*		1.441*		-4.308*		-2.830*	
SCOTLAND	-.581*		-.071		1.675*		-.034	

Table 28 (cont.)

VARIABLE	LNHOMIC				LNTHEFT			
	1960-1974		1975-1984		1960-1974		1975-1984	
	b	β	b	β	b	β	b	β
SINGAPORE	-.129		.004		.505*		.103	
SRILANKA	.725*		1.210*		-1.273*		-1.190*	
SYRIA	.863*		.316		-1.426*		-3.400*	
TURKEY	.933*		-		-1.067*		-	
ZAMBIA	.680*		.969*		1.170*		-	
R^2	.591		.651		.626		.798	
Adj. R^2	.561		.620		.598		.779	
N	501		198		499		280	

* $p<.05$.

After controlling for nation-specific effect of the non-core nations, Table 28 reveals that surplus value (SURPLUS) had a significant negative effect on theft in both time periods. Unemployment (UNEMP) had a significant negative effect on theft in the 1960-1974 period, but it had a positive one in the 1975-1984 period. Government expenditure (GOVEXP) had a significant positive effect on theft in both time periods. When I look at the nation-specific effects on theft, I found that (1) in the 1960-1974 period, Israel, Korea, Kuwait, Scotland, Singapore and Zambia had a significant positive effect on theft; (2) in the 1975-1984 period, the nation dummies for Israel and New Zealand were the only two which had significant positive effects on theft while the majority of the non-core nation dummies had a negative effect.

4) Comparisons of the OLS Estimations of the Separate and the Nested Theoretical Models Using Pooled data

Table 29 to Table 32 report the comparisons of the OLS estimations of the separate as well as the nested Durkheimian and Marxian models for homicide and theft in two pooled time periods. Model 1 and Model 2 represent the theoretical perspective separately: Model 1 includes only the Durkheimian explanatory variables and Model 2 includes only the Marxian explanatory variables. Model 3 to Model 5 are nested models. Model 3 includes both the Marxian and the Durkheimian perspectives, each serves as control for the other. Model 4 adds a common set of other control variables, i.e., FLABOR, DIVORCE and POP_1 to Model 3. Model 5 adds six interaction terms to Model 4. The interaction terms are constructed to test the following hypotheses: SD1, SD2 and SD3 laid out in the methodology (Chapter IV) section. The Synthesized Developmental Model predicts that the effects of economic development, urbanization and industrialization on crime depend on nations' world system location. There will be less criminogenic impact of economic development, urbanization and industrialization on crimes in Core nations than in Periphery and Semi-Periphery nations.

Before running my regression models including the interaction terms, I applied a centering method to avoid the problem of collinearity between the

Table 29:   Homicide (1960-1974): Comparisons of OLS Estimations of the Separate and Nested Theoretical Models Using Pooled Data (N =501, Standard Errors in Parentheses).

LNHOMIC (1960-1974)

	Model 1 b	Model 1 β	Model 2 b	Model 2 β	Model 3 b	Model 3 β	Model 4 b	Model 4 β	Model 5 b	Model 5 β
SURPLUS	-	-	.002*	.154*	.002*	.141*	.002*	.121*	.002	.110
	-		(.000)		(.000)		(.000)		(.000)	
UNEMP	-	-	.073*	.173*	.063*	.151*	.066*	.157*	.067*	.159*
	-		(.021)		(.021)		(.020)		(.020)	
SEMIPERI	-	-	.169	.098	.241*	.140*	.230*	.134*	.035	.021
	-		(.096)		(.108)		(.105)		(.130)	
PERIPH	-	-	.059	.033	.049	.027	.008	.004	.104	.057
	-		(.107)		(.125)		(.123)		(.128)	
GOVEXP	-	-	.002	.021	.007	.079	.006	.068	.005	.052
	-		(.004)		(.004)		(.004)		(.004)	
GROWTH_1	-.000	-.061	-	-	.000	.006	.000	.009	.000	.008
	(.000)		-		(.000)		(.000)		(.000)	
URBAN	.003*	.093*	-	-	.004*	.145*	.008*	.289*	.009*	.303*
	(.001)		-		(.002)		(.002)		(.002)	
INDUS	-1.051	-.095	-	-	.208	.019	.223	.020	1.037	.094
	(.560)		-		(.656)		(.644)		(.856)	
MORAL	-	-	-	-	-	-	-	-	-	-
	-		-		-		-		-	
DEMOC	-.047*	-.223*	-	-	-.035*	-.168*	-.034*	-.163*	-.033*	-.157*
	(.010)		-		(.012)		(.012)		(.012)	
FLABOR	-	-	-	-	-	-	-.006*	-.206*	-.005*	-.189*
	-		-		-		(.002)		(.002)	
DIVORCE	-	-	-	-	-	-	.030*	.096*	.028*	.092*
	-		-		-		(.013)		(.013)	
POP_1	-	-	-	-	-	-	-.000*	-.092*	-.000	-.051
	-		-		-		(.000)		(.000)	
GROWTH_1 x SEMIPERI	-	-	-	-	-	-	-	-	-.002*	-.171*
	-		-		-		-		(.000)	
GROWTH_1 x PERIPH	-	-	-	-	-	-	-	-	-.000	-.004
	-		-		-		-		(.000)	
URBAN x SEMIPERI	-	-	-	-	-	-	-	-	-.005	-.073
	-		-		-		-		(.004)	

Table 29 (cont.).

	LNHOMIC (1960-1974)								
	Model 1		Model 2		Model 3		Model 4		Model 5	
	b	β	b	β	b	β	b	β	b	β
URBAN x PERIPH	-	-	-	-	-	-	-	-	.000 (.004)	.000
INDUS x SEMIPERI	-	-	-	-	-	-	-	-	-3.400 (1.791)	-.104
INDUS x PERIPH	-	-	-	-	-	-	-	-	-.510 (1.577)	-.023
INTERCEPT	1.923*		.670*		.574		.620		.437	
R^2	.065*		.092*		.118*		.161*		.183*	
Adj. R^2	.058		.083		.101		.141		.153	
F (M1-M3)					5.883*					
F (M2-M3)					7.262*					
F (M3-M4)							8.481*			
F (M4-M5)									2.163	

* $p<.05$.
* Model 1-Durkheimian Perspective.
  Model 2-Marxian Perspective.
  Model 3-Model 1 + Model 2.

Model 4-Model 3 + Control Variables.
Model 5-Model 4 + Interaction Terms.

interaction term and the constituent variables in the interaction term (Roncek, 1996; Smith and Sasaki, 1979). I first subtract the means from the constituent variables and save their deviation scores. I then construct the interaction (product) terms based on the deviation scores of the constituent variables. I use hierarchical F-test to examine the incremental effect in the variances explained by different models.

Homicide: 1960-1974

The following observations are made from Table 29. First, model 1 shows that urbanization (URBAN) has a significant positive effect on homicide, while democracy (DEMOC) has a significant negative effect on homicide; (2) model 2 shows that both surplus value (SURPLUS) and unemployment (UNEMP) have a significant positive effect on homicide; (3) model 3 reveals that when combining explanatory variables from both perspectives, surplus value (SURPLUS), unemployment (UNEMP), semi-periphery nation status (SEMIPERI) and urbanization (URBAN) all have significant positive effects on homicide. Democracy (DEMOC) is the only variable that has a significant negative effect on homicide for the 1960-1974 period. F-tests indicate that significantly more variance was explained in the nested model including both theoretical perspectives. The R square for model 3 is .118, compared to the R square of .065 in model 1 and the R square of .092 in model 2; (4) model 4 adds additional control variables to model 3. It shows that the same observations made based on model 3 are sustained in model 4. The significant increase of the R squared from model 3 (R square equals to .118) to model 4 (R square equals to .161) implies that divorce (DIVORCE), female labor force participation (FLABOR) and population growth (POP_1) add significantly more variance explained to the model combining the Marxian and the Durkheimian perspectives; and (5) after adding six interaction terms to model 4, model 5 reveals that the significant effects of unemployment (UNEMP), urbanization (URBAN) and democracy (DEMOC) on homicide remain supportive of the relevant hypotheses. The observed significant effects of female labor force participation (FLABOR) and divorce (DIVORCE) on homicide from model 4 remain unchanged. Only one interaction term-GROWTH_1 x SEMIPERI has a significant effect on homicide. It indicates that those semi-periphery nations which have a higher economic growth rate have a lower homicide rate. Overall, adding interaction terms did not seem to improve the model fit statistics. The change of R squared from model 4 to model 5 is small and not significant.

Homicide: 1975-1984

Table 30 reports the OLS results of the separate and the nested Durkheimian and Marxian models on homicide for the 1975-1984 period. Model 1 indicates that moral individualism (MORAL) has a significant negative effect on homicide. Model 2 shows that unemployment (UNEMP), semi-periphery (SEMIPERI) and periphery (PERIPH) nation status and government expenditure (GOVEXP) all have a significant positive effect on homicide.

Model 3 shows that the significant effects of unemployment (UNEMP) and government expenditure (GOVEXP) and moral individualism (MORAL) on homicide from model 1 and model 2 remain unchanged in model 3. Model 3 also reveals that noticeable changes occurred after combining explanatory variables from both perspectives. First, semi-periphery (SEMIPERI) and periphery (PERIPH) nation status variables no longer have significant effects on homicide. Second, industrialization (INDUS) which had no significant effect on homicide in model 1 does have a significant negative effect on homicide in model 3. The R squared changes from model 1 to model 3 and from model 2 to model 3 indicate that significant more variance has been accounted for by combining the Marxian and the Durkheimian perspectives into the same model.

Model 4 shows that all observed significant effects in Model 3 remain unchanged after the three control variables were added. One of them, population growth (POP_1), has a significant positive effect on homicide. There is also a significant R squared increase from Model 3 to Model 4. In model 5, I observed that the significant effects of unemployment (UNEMP), government expenditure (GOVEXP) and population growth (POP_1) did not change. Nevertheless, after

Table 30: Homicide (1975-1984): Comparisons of OLS Estimations of the Separate and Nested Theoretical Models Using Pooled Data (N =198, Standard Errors in Parentheses).

LNHOMIC (1975-1984)

	Model 1		Model 2		Model 3		Model 4		Model 5	
	b	β	b	β	b	β	b	β	b	β
SURPLUS	-	-	.001	.061	-.003	-.133	-.000	-.029	.003	.149
	-		(.002)		(.002)		(.002)		(.002)	
UNEMP	-	-	.058*	.354*	.061*	.371*	.067*	.409*	.063*	.383*
	-		(.011)		(.011)		(.011)		(.015)	
SEMIPERI	-	-	.439*	.244*	.097	.054	.126	.070	.254	.141
	-		(.144)		(.159)		(.157)		(.171)	
PERIPH	-	-	.497*	.290*	.104	.061	.137	.079	.166	.097
	-		(.127)		(.145)		(.144)		(.133)	
GOVEXP	-	-	.016*	.232*	.016*	.239*	.022*	.319*	.027*	.388*
	-		(.005)		(.006)		(.006)		(.006)	
GROWTH_1	-.000	-.118	-	-	-.000	-.082	-.000	-.074	-.000	-.016
	(.000)		-		(.000)		(.000)		(.000)	
URBAN	.002	.053	-	-	-.000	-.032	.000	.000	.002	.059
	(.002)		-		(.002)		(.002)		(.002)	
INDUS	-.717	-.077	-	-	-1.529*	-.165*	-1.690*	-.182*	2.394*	.258*
	(.668)		-		(.747)		(.734)		(.970)	
MORAL	-.067*	-.304*	-	-	-.088*	-.401*	-.063*	-.288*	-.032	-.146
	(.016)		-		(.021)		(.022)		(.024)	
DEMOC	-	-	-	-	-	-	-	-	-	-
	-		-		-		-		-	
FLABOR	-	-	-	-	-	-	-.004	-.137	-.008*	-.254*
	-		-		-		(.003)		(.003)	
DIVORCE	-	-	-	-	-	-	-.010	-.035	-.018	-.063
	-		-		-		-		(.016)	
POP_1	-	-	-	-	-	-	.000*	.236*	.000*	.236*
	-		-		-		(.000)		(.000)	
GROWTH_1 x SEMIPERI	-	-	-	-	-	-	-	-	-.000	-.046
	-		-		-		-		(.000)	
GROWTH_1 x PERIPH	-	-	-	-	-	-	-	-	-.000	-.069
	-		-		-		-		(.000)	
URBAN x SEMIPERI	-	-	-	-	-	-	-	-	-.008	-.140
	-		-		-		-		(.004)	

	LNHOMIC (1975-1984)									
	Model 1		Model 2		Model 3		Model 4		Model 5	
	b	β	b	β	b	β	b	β	b	β
URBAN PERIPH	-	-	-	-	-	-	-	-	.010	.132
	-		-		-		-		(.007)	
INDUS SEMIPERI	-	-	-	-	-	-	-	-	-8.560*	-.413*
	-		-		-		-		(1.622)	
INDUS PERIPH	-	-	-	-	-	-	-	-	-7.710*	-.434*
	-		-		-		-		(1.800)	
INTERCEPT	2.530*		.310		2.151*		1.447*		-.370	
R^2	.135*		.238*		.328*		.372*		.520*	
adj. R^2	.117		.219		.296		.331		.472	
(M1-M3)					10.794*					
(M2-M3)					6.247*					
(M3-M4)							4.339*			
(M4-M5)									9.179*	

$p < .05$.

Model 1-Durkheimian Perspective.
Model 2-Marxian Perspective.
Model 3-Model 1 + Model 2.

Model 4-Model 3 + Control Variables.
Model 5-Model 4 + Interaction Terms.

adding six interaction terms to Model 4, the following changes occurred in Model 5: (1) the negative effect of industrialization (INDUS) on homicide in Model 4 has been changed to a positive one in Model 5; (2) moral individualism (MORAL) had a significant negative effect on homicide in Model 4, but it is no longer so in model 5; (3) the effect of female labor force participation (FLABOR) on homicide was not significant in Model 4 but it is significant in Model 5; and (4) two interaction terms have significant negative effects on homicide in Model 5: INDUS x SEMIPERI and INDUS x PERIPH. This indicates that for those semi-periphery and periphery nations, higher level of industrialization can lead to lower homicide rate. The F-test result comparing the R squares from Model 4 and Model 5 shows that significantly more variance has been explained in the model including interaction terms.

Theft: 1960-1974

Table 31 displays the results from five OLS regressions testing the separate as well as the nested theoretical models on theft in the 1960-1974 period. Model 1 shows that economic growth (GROWTH_1), industrialization (INDUS) and democracy (DEMOC) all have a significant positive effect on theft. About seventeen percent of the variance in theft was accounted for by the Durkheimian perspective alone. Model 2 reveals that both surplus value (SURPLUS) and unemployment (UNEMP) have significant negative effects on theft. Government expenditure (GOVEXP) has a significant positive effect on theft. The Marxian perspective alone accounts for about fifteen percent of the variance in theft.

Model 3 combines both theoretical perspectives. The following has been observed: (1) the effects of unemployment (UNEMP), industrialization (INDUS) and democracy (DEMOC) on theft changed little from the first two models to model 3; (2) the significant effects of surplus value (SURPLUS) and government expenditure (GOVEXP) on theft in Model 2 are no longer significant in Model 3; and (3) the overall variance explained increased significantly from both model 1 or Model 2 to Model 3. Approximately twenty-one percent of the variance in theft was accounted for in Model 3. Model 4 shows that adding three more control variables: female able 31: Theft (1960-1974): Comparisons of OLS Estimations of the Separate and Nested Theoretical Models Using Pooled Data (N =499, Standard Errors in Parentheses).

LNTHEFT (1960-1974)

	Model 1		Model 2		Model 3		Model 4		Model 5	
	b	β	b	β	b	β	b	β	b	β
URPLUS	-	-	-.004*	-.174*	-.001	-.055	-.001	-.059	-.001	-.056
	-		(.001)		(.001)		(.001)		(.001)	
NEMP	-	-	-.168*	-.230*	-.143*	-.196*	-.142*	-.195*	-.126*	-.173*
	-		(.035)		(.034)		(.034)		(.033)	
EMIPERI	-	-	-.081	-.028	.307	.106	.306	.106	.969*	.334*
	-		(.155)		(.175)		(.176)		(.197)	
ERIPH	-	-	-.150	-.048	.465*	.149*	.465*	.149*	.387	.124
	-		(.175)		(.205)		(.208)		(.206)	
OVEXP	-	-	.014*	.092*	.011	.071	.011	.069	.007	.047
	-		(.007)		(.007)		(.007)		(.007)	
ROWTH_1	.000*	.084*	-	-	.000	.047	.000	.047	.000	.082
	(.000)		-		(.000)		(.000)		(.000)	
RBAN	.003	.056	-	-	.005	.096	.005	.112	.011*	.212*
	(.003)		-		(.003)		(.003)		(.003)	
NDUS	2.582*	.135*	-	-	2.781*	.145*	2.751*	.144*	4.650*	.243*
	(.911)		-		(1.083)		(1.087)		(1.332)	
1ORAL	-	-	-	-	-	-	-	-	-	-
	-		-		-		-		-	
EMOC	.108*	.301*	-	-	.083*	.232*	.084*	.234*	.091*	.252
	(.017)		-		(.019)		(.019)		(.019)	
LABOR	-	-	-	-	-	-	-.000	-.017	-.000	-.007
	-		-		-		(.003)		(.003)	
IVORCE	-	-	-	-	-	-	.015	.029	.027	.054
	-		-		-		(.021)		(.020)	
OP_1	-	-	-	-	-	-	.000	.000	-.000*	-.105*
	-		-		-		(.000)		(.000)	
ROWTH_1 SEMIPERI	-	-	-	-	-	-	-	-	.004*	.268*
	-		-		-		-		(.000)	
ROWTH_1 PERIPH	-	-	-	-	-	-	-	-	-.000	-.057
	-		-		-		-		(.000)	
RBAN SEMIPERI	-	-	-	-	-	-	-	-	-.016*	-.119*
	-		-		-		-		(.007)	

Table 31 (cont.)

LNTHEFT (1960-1974)

	Model 1 b	β	Model 2 b	β	Model 3 b	β	Model 4 b	β	Model 5 b	β
URBAN x PERIPH	-	-	-	-	-	-	-	-	-.012	-.081
	-		-		-		-		(.008)	
INDUS x SEMIPERI	-	-	-	-	-	-	-	-	-2.941	-.053
	-		-		-		-		(2.801)	
INDUS x PERIPH	-	-	-	-	-	-	-	-	-6.790*	-.178*
	-		-		-		-		(2.444)	
INTERCEPT	4.048*		6.175*		4.287*		4.260*		3.463*	
R^2	.174*		.145*		.208*		.209*		.308*	
Adj. R^2	.167		.136		.194		.190		.282	
F (M1-M3)					4.709*					
F (M2-M3)					9.767*					
F (M3-M4)							.206			
F (M4-M5)									11.786*	

* $p<.05$.
* Model 1-Durkheimian Perspective.   Model 4-Model 3 + Control Variables.
  Model 2-Marxian Perspective.   Model 5-Model 4 + Interaction Terms.
  Model 3-Model 1 + Model 2.

labor force participation rate (FLABOR), divorce rate (DIVORCE) and population growth (POP_1) does not increase the R squared significantly. All the observed significant effects from Model 3 remain unchanged. The hierarchical F-test score was not statistically significant at the .05 level.

In Model 5, the significant effects of unemployment (UNEMP), industrialization (INDUS) and democracy (DEMOC) on theft are comparable to those found in Model 4. I find that: (1) semi-periphery nation status (SEMIPERI) and urbanization (URBAN) have positive effects on theft in Model 5 which were not observed in Model 4; (2) periphery nation status (PERIPH) which had a positive effect on theft in Model 4 is no longer significant in model 5; (3) population growth (POP_1) has a negative effect on theft in Model 5 which was not observed in Model 4; and (4) three interaction terms have significant effects on theft in Model 5. The interaction term of GROWTH_1 x SEMIPERI has a significant positive effect on theft which indicates that those semi-periphery nations that have higher economic growth rates also have higher theft rates. The interaction terms of URBAN x SEMIPERI and INDUS x PERIPH both have significant negative effects on theft. This means that in the 1960-1974 period (1) more urbanized semi-periphery nations had less theft, and (2) more industrialized periphery nations had less theft.

Theft: 1975-1984

Table 32 reports the regression estimates of the separate as well as the nested theoretical models on theft in the 1975-1984 period. Model 1 shows that economic growth (GROWTH_1), industrialization (INDUS) and moral individualism (MORAL) have significant positive effects on theft. About fifty-three percent of the variance in theft for the 1975-1984 period is accounted for by this Durkheimian model. Model 2 reveals that surplus value (SURPLUS), semi-periphery (SEMIPERI) and periphery (PERIPH) nation status have significant negative effects on theft. About forty-two percent of the variance in theft was accounted for by the Marxian perspective.

Table 32:   Theft (1975-1984): Comparisons of OLS Estimations of the Separate and Nested Theoretical Models Using Pooled Data (N = 280, Standard Errors in Parentheses).

LNTHEFT (1975-1984)

	Model 1		Model 2		Model 3		Model 4		Model 5	
	b	β	b	β	b	β	b	β	b	β
SURPLUS	-	-	-.016*	-.408*	-.009*	-.228*	-.016*	-.405*	-.016*	-.406*
			(.002)		(.002)		(.002)		(.002)	
UNEMP	-	-	.017	.044	.011	.027	-.002	-.006	-.001	-.004
			(.019)		(.018)		(.017)		(.018)	
SEMIPERI	-	-	-.815*	-.228*	.143	.040	.232	.065	-.119	-.033
			(.192)		(.194)		(.185)		(.192)	
PERIPH	-	-	-.997*	-.284*	.242	.069	.296	.084	.282	.083
			(.188)		(.215)		(.199)		(.194)	
GOVEXP	-	-	.013	.092	.005	.035	-.017*	-.116*	-.013	-.094
			(.007)		(.007)		(.007)		(.007)	
GROWTH_1	.000*	.096*	-	-	.000	.069	.000	.032	.000	.018
	(.000)				(.000)		(.000)		(.000)	
URBAN	-.000	-.000	-	-	-.000	-.007	-.004	-.067	-.007*	-.127*
	(.003)				(.003)		(.003)		(.003)	
INDUS	2.693*	.116*	-	-	2.682*	.116*	2.532*	.109*	-.818	-.035
	(1.014)				(1.137)		(1.049)		(1.534)	
MORAL	.300*	.663*	-	-	.259*	.572*	.231*	.510*	.181*	.400*
	(.020)				(.027)		(.026)		(.027)	
DEMOC	-	-	-	-	-	-	-	-	-	-
	-		-		-		-		-	
FLABOR	-	-	-	-	-	-	.006*	.109*	.007*	.126*
	-		-		-		(.003)		(.003)	
DIVORCE	-	-	-	-	-	-	-.009	-.016	.003	.005
	-		-		-		(.023)		(.023)	
POP_1	-	-	-	-	-	-	-.000*	-.309*	-.000*	-.289*
	-		-		-		(.000)		(.000)	
GROWTH_1 x SEMIPERI	-	-	-	-	-	-	-	-	.000	.059
	-		-		-		-		(.000)	
GROWTH x PERIPH	-	-	-	-	-	-	-	-	.000	.026
	-		-		-		-		(.000)	
URBAN x SEMIPERI	-	-	-	-	-	-	-	-	.011	.084
	-		-		-		-		(.006)	

	LNTHEFT (1975-1984)									
	Model 1		Model 2		Model 3		Model 4		Model 5	
	b	β	b	β	b	β	b	β	b	β
RBAN PERIPH	-	-	-	-	-	-	-	-	-.000	-.005
	-		-		-		-		(.006)	
NDUS SEMIPERI	-	-	-	-	-	-	-	-	.219	.005
	-		-		-		-		(2.347)	
NDUS PERIPH	-	-	-	-	-	-	-	-	11.530*	.269*
	-		-		-		-		(2.551)	
NTERCEPT	3.016*		8.135*		4.037*		6.129*		7.395*	
R^2	.527*		.419*		.570*		.639*		.675*	
dj. R^2	.520		.409		.556		.623		.652	
(M1-M3)					5.726*					
(M2-M3)					23.682*					
(M3-M4)							17.005*			
(M4-M5)									4.800*	

$p<.05$.

Model 1-Durkheimian Perspective.
Model 2-Marxian Perspective.
Model 3-Model 1 + Model 2.

Model 4-Model 3 + Control Variables.
Model 5-Model 4 + Interaction Terms.

Model 3 is the nested model which combines both the Marxian and the Durkheimian perspectives. I find that the significant effects of semi-periphery (SEMIPERI) and periphery (PERIPH) nation status variables on theft in Model 2 no longer exist in Model 3. Economic growth (GROWTH_1) is significant in Model 1 but it is not significant in Model 3. The effects of surplus value (SURPLUS), industrialization (INDUS) and moral individualism (MORAL) on theft appear to be stable across different models. The overall fit statistics shows that about fifty-seven percent of the variance in theft was accounted for by the Model 3. Model 4 indicates that adding another three control variables increases R squared significantly, i.e., from .57 in Model 3 to .64 in Model 4. The following is observed (1) the effects of surplus value (SURPLUS), industrialization (INDUS) and moral individualism (MORAL) on theft in Model 3 and Model 4 are still comparable; (2) the effect of government expenditure (GOVEXP) on theft was not significant in Model 3, but it has a significant negative effect on theft in Model 4; (3) female labor force participation (FLABOR) has a significant positive effect on theft; and (4) population growth (POP_1) has a significant negative effect on theft.

In Model 5, the effects of the following variables on theft remain unchanged compared to those observed in Model 4: surplus value (SURPLUS), moral individualism (MORAL), female labor force participation (FLABOR) and population growth (POP_1).

The significant effects of government expenditure (GOVEXP) and industrialization (INDUS) on theft in Model 4 do not exist in Model 5. Urbanization (URBAN) has a significant effect on theft in Model 5 which was not observed in Model 4. The interaction term, INDUS x PERIPH, has a significant positive effect on theft which indicates that the more industrialized periphery nations have a higher theft rate. In Model 5, about sixty-eight percent of the variance is explained, compared to sixty-four percent explained in Model 4. The change of R squared is statistically significant.

Summary

In this rather lengthy section, I provided detailed description of the results from regression models testing both the Durkheimian and the Marxian perspectives using pooled data. First of all, the separate OLS estimations of each of the two theoretical perspectives provide valuable base line information for the later analysis and discussion. Secondly, I ran Weighted Least Squares (WLS) analysis for selected models to get rid of the heteroskedasticity problem. I found that the results from either OLS or WLS are similar. Third, I applied the Least Square Dummy Variable (LSDV) technique to explore country-specific effects on crime. I listed countries which exhibit abnormal characteristics compared to their peers. For example, the nation dummy variables for the United States, Italy and France had a significant positive effect on homicide while those for the rest of the developed nation had a negative effect on homicide in the 1960-1974 period. Therefore, findings concerning the nation-specific effects can be helpful for identifying targets for qualitative study. Lastly, the comparison between separate and nested models is useful to test the strength and consistency of the theoretical effects.

Chapter VII

Comparisons and Contrasts: Past, Present and Future of Comparative
Criminological Research Based on Marxian and Durkheimian Perspectives

Theoretical Implications

Is there a single process which produces both homicide and theft?

Previous comparative research has attempted to find out whether there is a
single causal process which produces both homicide and theft. LaFree (1997)
identifies fourteen studies in the past three decades which have examined both
homicide and theft at the same time. Thirteen of them find no support that homicide
and theft are produced by a single process (Bennett, 1991; Hartnagel, 1982; Kick and
LaFree, 1985; Krohn, 1976, 1978; Krohn and Wellford, 1977; LaFree and Kick,
1986; Landau, 1984; McDonald, 1976; Neapolitan, 1996; Steffensmeier et al., 1989;
Wellford, 1974; Wolf, 1971). Using a pooled cross-sectional time-series data, Ortega
et al.'s (1992) study is the only exception which found a significant positive effect of
economic development on both homicide and theft.

Table 33 illustrates the findings of the bivariate correlations between the
explanatory variables and the crime variables in my study. I find that none of the

significant correlations between an explanatory variable and each of the crime variables have a consistent direction, either positive or negative. This observation is applicable to all time periods in both the cross-sectional and the pooled analysis. In short, I find no evidence from correlation analysis to suggest that homicide and theft are produced by a single causal process.

Table 34 summarizes the regression results of each of the two theoretical perspectives using both the cross-sectional and the pooled data. I ran the Marxian and the Durkheimian model separately without controlling for each other, nor controlling for additional variables. Again, none of the explanatory variables has the same significant effect on both homicide and theft, rejecting the notion that homicide and theft are produced by a single process.

Comparison of the Theoretical Relationships with Previous Research

In this section, I compare my regression results from both the cross-sectional and the pooled analysis to the relevant findings from previous cross-national studies. Hypothesized theoretical relationships derived from both the Durkheimian and the Marxian perspective are discussed separately. Table 34 is the reference table for the discussions in this section.

1) Economic Growth, Industrialization and Crime

Economic development and industrialization are among the most popular variables included in previous comparative research on crime. Economic development is often measured as the GNP or GDP per capita (Braithwaite and Braithwaite, 1980; Fiala and LaFree, 1988; Groves et al., 1985; Hansmann and Quigley, 1982; Hartnagel, 1982; Krahn et al., 1986; Krohn, 1976; Krohn and Wellford, 1977; McDonald, 1976; Messner, 1980, 1982, 1985; Neapolitan, 1994, 1996; Wellford, 1974; Wolf, 1971). Industrialization is often measured as the proportion of the work force in agricultural jobs (Bennett, 1991; Groves et al., 1985; Krahn et al., 1986; Wolf, 1971), or energy consumption per capita (Avison and Loring, 1986; Conklin and Simpson, 1985; Krohn, 1976, 1978).

Table 33:   Summary of Predicted and the Observed Correlational Relationship Between Crimes and Independent Variables.

	Predicted	Observed												
		Homicide							Theft					
		Cross-Sectional Data					Pooled Data		Cross-Sectional Data				Pooled Data	
		60-64	65-69	70-74	75-79	80-84	60-74	75-84	65-69	70-74	75-79	80-84	60-74	75-84
UNEMP	+	+*	+	+*	+	+*	+*	+*	-	-	-	-	-*	-
SURPLUS	+	+*	+*	+	+	+	+*	+	-*	-*	-*	-*	-*	-*
GOVEXP	-	-	-	-	+	+	-	+	+	+	+*	+*	+*	+*
PERIPH	+	+	+	-	+	+	+*	+*	-	-*	-*	-*	-*	-*
SEMIPERI	+	+	+	+	+	-	+*	+	-	-	-*	-	-*	-*
URBAN	+	-	+	+	+	+	-	-	+*	+*	+	+	+*	+*
INDUS	+	-	-*	-	-	-	-*	-*	+*	+*	+	+*	+*	+*
GROWTH_1	+	-	-*	-*	+	-*	+	-*	+	+*	+*	+	+*	+*
MORAL	-	n.a.	n.a.	n.a.	-	-*	n.a.	-*	n.a.	n.a.	+*	+*	n.a.	+*
DEMOC	-	-*	-	-*	n.a.	n.a.	-*	n.a.	+*	+*	n.a.	n.a.	+*	n.a.

* p < .05.

Table 34:   Summary of Regression Results from the Cross-Sectional and the Pooled Data.

	Predicted	Observed													
		Homicide							Theft						
		Cross-Sectional Data					Pooled Data		Cross-Sectional Data					Pooled Data	
		60-64	65-69	70-74	75-79	80-84	60-74	75-84	60-64	65-69	70-74	75-79	80-84	60-74	75-84
UNEMP	+	+*	+*	+*	+	+*	+*	+*	-	-	+	-	-	-*	+
SURPLUS	+	+	+*	+	+	+	+*	+	-*	-*	-	-*	-*	-*	-*
GOVEXP	-	-	+	+	+	+	+	+*	+	-	+	-	-	+*	+
PERIPH	+	+	-	-	+	-	+	+*	+	-	-	+	-	-	-*
SEMIPERI	+	+	-	-	+	-	+	+*	+	+	-	+	-	-	-*
URBAN	+	+*	+	+*	+	+	+*	+	-	+	+	+	+	+	-
INDUS	+	-	-*	-	-	+	-	-	+	+	+	-	+	+*	+*
GROWTH_1	+	+*	+	-	+	-*	-	-	+*	+*	+	+	+	+*	+*
MORAL	-	n.a.	n.a.	n.a.	-*	-*	n.a.	-*	n.a.	n.a.	n.a.	+*	+*	n.a.	+*
DEMOC	-	-*	+	-	n.a.	n.a.	-*	n.a.	+	+*	+	n.a.	n.a.	+*	n.a.

* p < .05.

Despite the differences in measurement of these two variables, the majority of the previous comparative studies find either null or negative effect of economic development or industrialization on homicide (LaFree, 1997). Ortega et al.'s (1992) study is the only exception, where a significant positive effect of industrialization on homicide was found. It is worth noting that Ortega et al.'s (1992) findings came from a pooled time-series analysis. In my cross-sectional analysis, I find a significant negative effect of economic growth on homicide in the 1980-1984 period. I also find a significant negative effect of industrialization on homicide in the 1965-1969 period. In my pooled time series analysis, I did not find any significant effect of either economic growth or industrialization on homicide.

Compared to the studies on homicide, only a limited number of studies have examined the effect of economic development and industrialization on theft. Most of them find a significant positive effect of economic development and industrialization on theft (Hartnagel, 1982; Krohn, 1976, 1978; Krohn and Wellford, 1977; Stack, 1984; Wellford, 1974). Kick and LaFree (1985) and McDonald (1976) did not find evidence that property crime increases with industrialization and economic development.

I find a consistent significant positive effect of economic growth and industrialization on theft in both pooled time periods: 1960-1974 and 1975-1984. Economic growth also has a significant positive effect on theft in one of the five cross-sectional time period: 1960-1964. In sum, my findings on economic growth, industrialization, and crime are consistent with the bulk of previous research.

2) Urbanization and Crime

Many previous cross-national studies have examined the relationship between urbanization and crime. It is hypothesized that more urbanized nations are likely to have higher crime rates. Research findings, however, are often mixed. Using population growth rate as measurement of urbanization, two studies have found a positive effect of urbanization on homicide (Krahn et al., 1986; McDonald, 1976) but two others did not (Messner, 1982; Krohn and Wellford, 1977). Both Krohn and

Wellford (1977) and McDonald (1976) found a significant positive effect of urbanization on theft.

Most cross-national studies which operationalize urbanization as the percentage of the population living in urban areas did not find a significant positive effect of urbanization on either homicide (Avison and Loring, 1986; Conklin and Simpson, 1985; Hansmann and Quigley, 1982; Hartnagel, 1982; Kick and LaFree, 1985; Krohn, 1978; Messner, 1980; Ortega et al., 1992; Wellford, 1974) or theft (Hartnagel, 1982; Kick and LaFree, 1985; Wellford, 1974). In fact, some studies suggest that there is a significant negative effect of urbanization on homicide (Conklin and Simpson, 1985; Quinney, 1965; Wolf, 1971; Krohn, 1978; Ortega et al., 1992).

I operationalize urbanization as the yearly percentage of a nation's population residing in urban areas. Consistent with previous research, my findings are mixed. Results from my cross-sectional analysis indicate that (1) urbanization has a significant positive effect on homicide in two cross-sectional data time periods: 1960-1964 and 1970-1974 and (2) there is no significant effect of urbanization on theft in any of the cross-sectional time periods. In my pooled analysis, urbanization has a significant positive effect on homicide in the 1960-1974 period. There is no significant effect of urbanization on theft in any of the pooled time periods.

3) Moral Individualism and Crime

Only a handful of comparative studies have looked into the effect of moral individualism on homicide. Messner (1982) uses Protestant religiosity and school enrollment as measurements of moral individualism. He did not find a relationship between these two measures and homicide. Huang (1995) operationalizes moral individualism as including two factors: individualism and communitarianism. Individualism is measured by the sum of the scores of political and civil rights. Communitarianism is measured as the percentages of government expenditures for social security and health care. Huang (1995) found a significant negative effect of individualism on homicide but no significant effect of communitarianism on homicide. He suggests that a society's common sentiment of respect for individuals' political and civil rights inhibit citizens from killing each other. Neapolitan (1995) tested the effect of political rights on theft in a sample including only the less developed nations. He found that political rights had a significant positive effect on theft in less developed nations.

I measure moral individualism as the sum of political and civil rights. I use moral individualism as an indicator for the Durkheimian civilization concept. In both cross-sectional and pooled analysis, my study finds a consistent significant negative effect of moral individualism on homicide in all but the 1965-1969 periods. I also find a significant positive effect of moral individualism on theft in all but the 1960-1964 periods.

4) Surplus Value and Crime

To my knowledge, the effect of surplus value on crime has not been tested in any previous cross-national studies. Lynch et al.'s (1994) time series analysis using United States crime data from 1950 to 1974 reveals that (1) the effect of surplus value on crime precedes that of unemployment on crime in Marxist theory. When the surplus value variable is controlled in the regression model, unemployment rate either has no significant effect on crime, or the effect is negative when significant; (2) surplus value is a significant predictor of the rate of property crime known, property crime arrests, violent crime known, violent crime arrests and total index crimes known to police in the United States from 1950 to 1974; and (3) all the observed effects of surplus value are positive. The authors suggest that the relationship between surplus value and crime needs to be tested in other countries and in other time periods.

My study includes both surplus value and unemployment in the same Marxian model. I find that the effect of surplus value on homicide is consistently positive. It is significant, however, only for two time periods: 1965-1969 in the cross-sectional analysis and 1960-1974 in the pooled analysis. Interestingly, the effect of surplus value on theft is a negative one and is significant in all but one time periods: 1970-1974.

5) Unemployment and Crime

Some cross-national studies have tested the effect of unemployment on crime. Fiala and LaFree (1988) find no significant effect of unemployment on child homicides. McDonald's (1976) study also did not find any significant effect of unemployment on homicide. Neapolitan (1995) finds no evidence to suggest that unemployment has any significant effect on theft in less developed nations. Although a positive bivariate correlation relationship between unemployment and homicide has been found by Avison and Loring (1986) and by Krohn (1976), the significant correlation found in both studies disappeared when other measures were controlled in multivariate analysis.

Unlike most of the previous cross-national research, I find a significant positive effect of unemployment on homicide in all but the 1975-1979 time periods. The effect of unemployment on homicide appears stable even when controlling for surplus value. The effect of unemployment on theft is less consistent and is negative. The significant negative effect of unemployment on theft, however, was found only in the 1960-1974 period using pooled data.

6) Government Expenditure and Crime

DeFronzo (1997:396) summarizes a few cross-national studies that have used government expenditure to predict crime. Fiala and LaFree (1988) found a significant negative effect of welfare spending on child homicide victimization among eighteen industrialized nations. Similarly, using advanced industrialized nations as sample, Gartner (1990, 1991) and Briggs and Cutright (1994) both found a significant negative effect of "social assistance" on child homicide. Pampel and Gartner (1995) also found that the level of welfare assistance had a significant negative effect on homicide offending among young men in eighteen industrialized nations. A significant negative effect of welfare assistance on property crime has been found in single nation studies (DeFronzo, 1983, 1996; Devine et al., 1988).

I measure the theoretical concept-human investment as the total percentage of the government expenditures in social security, social welfare, health care and education in this study. Contrary to expectations, my cross-sectional analysis results indicate no significant effect of government expenditure on social welfare, on either homicide or theft. Also contrary to expectations, in my pooled analysis, I found a significant positive effect of government expenditure on homicide in the 1975-1984 period as well as a significant positive effect on theft in the 1960-1974 period.

7) World System Location and Crime

Lynch et al. (1988) tested a hypothesis which proposes that the rates of violent and property crime will differ according to world system location. Core nations will have higher rates of property crime because of the democratic and egalitarian ideologies. Periphery countries will have higher rates of violent crime due to political repression, frustration-aggression reactions and alienation. Controlling for income inequality and the level of economic development, Lynch et al.'s (1988) study finds support for their hypotheses regarding crimes in the core and the periphery nations. The patterns for semi-periphery nations, however, are not clear.

I constructed two dummy variables: Semi-periphery nations (SEMIPERI) and Periphery nations (PERIPH) to depict position in the world system. The core nations are held as the reference group. I did not find any significant effect of SEMIPERI and PERIPH on crime in my cross-sectional analysis. In my pooled analysis, however, I found a significant positive effect of both SEMIPERI and PERIPH on homicide in the 1975-1984 period. I also found a significant negative effect of both SEMIPERI and PERIPH on theft in the 1975-1984 period.

Genuine or Spurious Effect?

Because of the usual small sample size, many earlier cross-national studies have not been able to control for possible spurious effects, e.g., effects of some theoretical variables on crime can be substantially changed once other rival variables are controlled. Researchers have called for including a common set of controls to examine the genuine effect of theoretical variables (Neuman and Berger, 1988). In my study, I am able to test for possible spurious effects by using nested models including a common set of control variables. Table 35 and Table 36 summarize my findings comparing results from separate theoretical models and those from nested models. In both tables, Model 1 includes variables from the Durkheimian perspective. Model 2 includes variables from the Marxian perspective. Model 3 includes variables from both the Durkheimian and the Marxian perspectives. Model 4 adds a common set of other control variables to Model 3. Model 5 adds interaction terms to Model 4. Comparing findings between nested models is helpful to future theory construction and testing.

In Table 35, if I look at Model 3 first, I find that the following findings from Model 1 and Model 2 remain unchanged in Model 3 (1) the significant positive effect of unemployment on homicide in both the 1960-1974 and the 1975-1984 periods; (2) the significant positive effect of surplus value and urbanization on homicide in the 1960-1974 period; (3) the significant positive effect of government expenditure on homicide in the 1975-1984 period; and (4) the significant negative effect of moral individualism or democracy on homicide in the 1960-1974 and the 1975-1984 periods. The positive effect of semi-periphery nation status on homicide in the 1960-1974 period was not significant in Model 2 but it is in Model 3. The negative effect of industrialization on homicide was not significant in Model 2 but it is in Model 3.

All the significant effects observed in Model 3 in Table 35 remain unchanged in Model 4 when additional control variables (DIVORCE, FLABOR and POP_1) are added. Observable changes did occur in Model 5 when six interaction terms are introduced. These interaction terms were constructed from hypotheses about the differences in the criminogenic impact of economic growth, urbanization and industrialization on crime in periphery and semi-periphery nations compared to that in core nations. Results from Model 5 indicate that the significant effects of unemployment, government expenditure, urbanization and democracy on homicide from Model 4 remain unchanged. However, the significant positive effects of surplus

Table 35:   Changing Effects of the Independent Variables on Homicide Using Pooled Data by Model.

	Predicted	Model 1 T1	Model 1 T2	Model 2 T1	Model 2 T2	Model 3 T1	Model 3 T2	Model 4 T1	Model 4 T2	Model 5 T1	Model 5 T2
						HOMICIDE					
UNEMP	+	n.a.	n.a.	+*	+*	+*	+*	+*	+*	+*	+*
SURPLUS	+	n.a.	n.a.	+*	-	+*	-	+*	-	+	+
SEMIPERI	+	n.a.	n.a.	+	+	+*	+	+*	+	+	+
PERIPH	+	n.a.	n.a.	+	+	+	+	+	+	+	+
GOVEXP	-	n.a.	n.a.	+	+*	+	+*	+	+*	+	+*
GROWTH_1	+	-	-	n.a.	n.a.	+	-	+	-	+	-
URBAN	+	+*	+	n.a.	n.a.	+*	-	+*	+	+*	+
INDUS	+	-	-	n.a.	n.a.	+	-*	+	-*	+	+*
MORAL	-	n.a.	-*	n.a.	n.a.	n.a.	-*	n.a.	-*	n.a.	-
DEMOC	-	-*	n.a.	n.a.	n.a.	-*	n.a.	-*	n.a.	-*	n.a.
FLABOR	n.a.	n.a.	n.a.	n.a.	n.a.	n.a.	n.a.	-*	-	-*	-*
DIVORCE	n.a.	n.a.	n.a.	n.a.	n.a.	n.a.	n.a.	+*	-	+*	-

Table 35 (cont.)

	Predicted	Model 1 T1	Model 1 T2	Model 2 T1	Model 2 T2	Model 3 T1	Model 3 T2	Model 4 T1	Model 4 T2	Model 5 T1	Model 5 T2
POP_1	n.a.	n.a.	n.a.	n.a.	n.a.	n.a.	n.a.	-*	+*	-	+*
GROWTH_1 x SEMIPERI	+	n.a.	n.a.	n.a.	n.a.	n.a.	n.a.	n.a.	n.a.	-*	-
GROWTH_1 x PERIPH	+	n.a.	n.a.	n.a.	n.a.	n.a.	n.a.	n.a.	n.a.	-	-
URBAN x SEMIPERI	+	n.a.	n.a.	n.a.	n.a.	n.a.	n.a.	n.a.	n.a.	-	-
URBAN x PERIPH	+	n.a.	n.a.	n.a.	n.a.	n.a.	n.a.	n.a.	n.a.	+	+
INDUS x SEMIPERI	+	n.a.	n.a.	n.a.	n.a.	n.a.	n.a.	n.a.	n.a.	-	-*
INDUS x PERIPH	+	n.a.	n.a.	n.a.	n.a.	n.a.	n.a.	n.a.	n.a.	-	-*

* p <.05.
* Model 1-Durkheimian Perspective.
Model 2-Marxian Perspective.
Model 3-Model 1 + Model 2.
Model 4-Model 3 + Control Variables.
Model 5-Model 4 + Interactions Terms.
* T1: 1960-1974; T2: 1975-1984.

value, semi-periphery nation status and moral individualism in Model 4 are no longer significant in Model 5 for the same time period. The significant negative effect of industrialization for the 1975-1984 period in Model 4 became a significant positive one in Model 5 when interaction terms are included.

Three interaction terms have significant effects on homicide. The interaction term, GROWTH_1 x SEMIPERI, has a significant negative effect on homicide in the 1960-1974 period. This indicates that a higher rate of economic growth in semi-periphery nations during the 1960-1975 period is associated with lower homicide rate. The interactions terms of INDUS x SEMIPERI and INDUS x PERIPH both have significant negative effects on homicide in the 1975-1984 period. This indicates that in those semi-periphery or periphery nations, higher level of industrialization is associated with lower rate of homicide in the 1975-1984 period.

Table 36 reveals that the observed significant effects of surplus value, industrialization, moral individualism and democracy on theft from Model 1 or Model 2 remain the same in Model 3. The significant negative effect of unemployment on theft and the significant positive effect of government expenditure on theft in the 1960-1974 period in Model 2 are no longer significant in Model 3. Periphery nation status which does not have a significant effect on theft in Model 2 now has a significant positive effect in the 1960-1974 period in Model 3.

I find that the significant effects of industrialization, moral individualism and democracy on theft in both time periods observed in Model 3 still hold true in Model 4 when additional control variables are included. In Model 4, the results show that unemployment has a significant negative effect on theft in the 1960-1974 period which was not found in Model 3. The effect of surplus value on theft was significant in both pooled time periods in Model 3, but it is only significant in the 1975-1984 period in Model 4. Government expenditure on social welfare which has no significant effect on theft in any of the two time periods in Model 3, has a significant negative effect on theft in the 1975-1984 period in Model 4.

Table 36: Changing Effects of the Independent Variables on Theft Using Pooled Data by Model.

	Predicted	THEFT									
		Model 1		Model 2		Model 3		Model 4		Model 5	
		T1	T2	T1	T2	T1	T2	T1	T2	T1	T2
UNEMP	+	n.a.	n.a.	-*	+	-	+	-*	-	-*	-
SURPLUS	+	n.a.	n.a.	-*	-*	-*	-*	-	-*	-	-*
SEMIPERI	+	n.a.	n.a.	-	+	+	+	+	+	+*	-
PERIPH	+	n.a.	n.a.	-	+	+*	+	+*	+	+	+
GOVEXP	-	n.a.	n.a.	+*	+	+	+	+	-*	+	-
GROWTH_1	+	+*	+*	n.a.	n.a.	+	+	+	+	+	+
URBAN	+	+	-	n.a.	n.a.	+	-	+	-	+*	-*
INDUS	+	+*	+*	n.a.	n.a.	+*	+*	+*	+*	+*	-
MORAL	-	n.a.	+*	n.a.	n.a.	n.a.	+*	n.a.	+*	n.a.	+*
DEMOC	-	+*	n.a.	n.a.	n.a.	+*	n.a.	+*	n.a.	+*	n.a.
FLABOR	n.a.	n.a.	n.a.	n.a.	n.a.	n.a.	n.a.	-	+*	-	+*
DIVORCE	n.a.	n.a.	n.a.	n.a.	n.a.	n.a.	n.a.	+	-	+	+

Table 36 (cont.)

Predicted	Model 1 T1	Model 1 T2	Model 2 T1	Model 2 T2	Model 3 T1	Model 3 T2	Model 4 T1	Model 4 T2	Model 5 T1	Model 5 T2
POP_1 n.a.	n.a.	n.a.	n.a.	n.a.	n.a.	n.a.	+	-*	-*	-*
GROWTH_1 x SEMIPERI +	n.a.	n.a.	n.a.	n.a.	n.a.	n.a.	n.a.	n.a.	+*	+
GROWTH_1 x PERIPH +	n.a.	n.a.	n.a.	n.a.	n.a.	n.a.	n.a.	n.a.	-	+
URBAN x SEMIPERI +	n.a.	n.a.	n.a.	n.a.	n.a.	n.a.	n.a.	n.a.	-*	+
URBAN x PERIPH +	n.a.	n.a.	n.a.	n.a.	n.a.	n.a.	n.a.	n.a.	-	-
INDUS x SEMIPERI +	n.a.	n.a.	n.a.	n.a.	n.a.	n.a.	n.a.	n.a.	-	+
INDUS x PERIPH +	n.a.	n.a.	n.a.	n.a.	n.a.	n.a.	n.a.	n.a.	-*	+*

* $p < .05$.
* Model 1-Durkheimian Perspective.
Model 2-Marxian Perspective.
Model 3-Model 1 + Model 2.
Model 4-Model 3 + Control Variables.
Model 5-Model 4 + Interaction Terms.
* T1: 1960-1974; T2: 1975-1984.

Some observed effects from Model 4 changed again in Model 5 which includes interaction terms. The significant effects of unemployment, surplus value, moral individualism and democracy on theft are the only ones that stay the same in both Model 4 and Model 5. Semi-periphery nation status and urbanization had no significant effect on theft in any of the previous models. However, both have significant effects on theft in Model 5. Semi-periphery nation status has a significant positive effect on theft in the 1960-1974 period. The effect of urbanization on theft is a positive one in the 1960-1974 period, but a negative one in the 1975-1984 period. The effect of industrialization was significant in both time periods in model 4 but it is only significant in the 1960-1974 period in model 5.

Three interactions terms have a significant effect on theft. GROWTH_1 x SEMIPERI has a significant positive effect on theft in the 1960-1984 period which indicates that the rate of economic growth in semi-periphery nations is related to higher theft rate. The significant negative effect of URBAN x SEMIPERI in the 1960-1974 period indicates that semi-periphery nations that are more urbanized have lower theft rates in that time period. The effect of INDUS x PERIPH on theft is negative in the 1960-1974 period but is positive in the 1975-1984 period. This indicates a possible changing effect of industrialization on theft in the periphery nations across different time periods.

Conclusion

When the Durkheimian and the Marxian perspective were tested separately, my findings are comparable to those from previous cross-national studies. First, I did not find evidence to suggest that there is a single process which produce both homicide and theft. Second, regression results indicate that some of my theoretical variables have more consistent effects on homicide or theft compared to others. For example, from the Marxian perspective, unemployment (UNEMP) and surplus value (SURPLUS) both have consistent positive effects on homicide. Surplus value (SURPLUS) has consistent negative effects on theft. From the Durkheimian perspective, urbanization (URBAN) has consistent positive effects while moral individualism (MORAL) or democracy (DEMOC) have consistent negative effects on homicide. Industrialization (INDUS), economic growth (GROWTH_1), moral individualism (MORAL) and democracy (DEMOC) all have consistent positive effects on theft.

When nested models are used, observable changes occur. However, some theoretical effects appear to be strong and stable. In my most strict model (model 5), I included variables from both the Durkheimian and the Marxian perspectives and added three control variables and six interaction terms. I find that theoretical variables such as unemployment (UNEMP), government expenditure on social welfare (GOVEXP), urbanization (URBAN), industrialization (INDUS) and democracy (DEMOC) are still significant predictors of homicide and most of these variables are also significant predictors of theft.

It is evident that there are fluctuations in the observed theoretical relationships across different time periods and in different regression models. I argue that some of these may very well be the consequences of sample composition. Sample composition can change parameter estimates of the slopes and intercepts significantly. Furthermore, it may be of practical value to know how a theory applies to different samples. The following provide a discussion of the impact of sample composition.

Methodological Implications

The Impact of Sample Composition

Neuman and Berger (1988) argue that sample composition in comparative studies may affect the results far more than has previously been recognized. I have observed from the descriptive statistics presented in table 3 that there are apparent differences between sub-sample groups in the means and standard deviations of the variables included. I have also provided a partial test of this proposition in my regression analysis. Using the pooled data, I break my sample into different groups in testing different theoretical perspectives across two time periods: 1960-1974 and 1975-1984. For the Durkheimian perspective, the comparisons are between two sub-sample groups: developed nations vs. developing nations. For the Marxian perspective, the two sub-sample groups are (1) core nations; and (2) non-core nations. Table 37 outlines the major findings presented in table 20 to table 23.

From a first look of the results, I find that the differences in signs and in significance of regression coefficients between different sub-samples are obvious. For example, in the 1960-1974 period, the Durkheimian model on homicide using the developed nation sub-sample shows that (1) both urbanization (URBAN) and industrialization (INDUS) have significant positive effects on homicide; and (2) democracy (DEMOC) has a significant negative effect on homicide. All these observations are supportive of the Durkheimian hypotheses. Using the developing nation sub-sample to test the same model for the same time period, however, produces different results. In fact, none of the explanatory variables have any significant effect on homicide. Thus, to generalize the findings obtained from the regression analysis using the developed nation sub-sample to the developing nations is not appropriate.

Interestingly, there is a new twist to my findings. It appears that the impact of sample composition on the regression results may not be equally applicable to different theoretical perspectives. For example, I find that unemployment (UNEMP) has a significant effect on homicide in the 1975-1984 period, regardless of the different sub-sample I used. Similar observations can be found with regard to the effect of unemployment (UNEMP) on theft in the 1960-1975 period and the effect of surplus value (SURPLUS) on theft in both pooled time periods. This suggests that explanatory variables from the Marxian perspective are more likely to withstand the impact of different sample composition compared to those from the Durkheimian perspective. Moral individualism (MORAL) is the only variable from the Durkheimian perspective which has a significant positive effect on theft in both of

Table 37: Homicide and Theft: Comparing Different Sub-sample Groups (Developed vs. Developing Nations or Core vs. Non-Core Nations) Using Pooled Data by Time Period.

	Predicted	HOMICIDE				THEFT			
		1960-1974		1975-1984		1960-1974		1975-1984	
		I	II	I	II	I	II	I	II
GROWTH_1	+	+	-	-	-	+	+	+	+
URBAN	+	+*	+	+	+*	+	-	-	+
INDUS	+	+*	+	+*	-*	+*	+	+	+
MORAL	-	n.a.	n.a.	+*	-*	n.a.	n.a.	+*	+*
DEMOC	-	-*	-	n.a.	n.a.	+*	+	n.a.	n.a.
UNEMP	+	+*	-	+*	+*	-*	-*	+*	-
SURPLUS	+	+	+*	-	+*	-*	-*	-*	-*
GOVEXP	-	-	+	+*	-*	+*	-	+*	+

* p < .05.
* I: Regression model using developed nation or core nation sub-sample.
II: Regression model using developing nation or non-core nation sub-sample.

178

the pooled time periods, regardless of the different sub-sample used.

My tentative conclusion is that the impact of sample composition on regression results are likely to exist. I suggest the use of interaction terms to capture the changes in the regression slopes when a particular theory allows one to suspect such an impact based on different sample characteristics. For example, in my study, the Durkheimian hypotheses do not differentiate the effect of economic growth, urbanization, industrialization and moral individualism on crime based on sample characteristics such as the level of development (developed vs. developing). On the other hand, the world system dimension of the Marxian perspective does allow us to consider the interactive effect of the economic growth, urbanization and industrialization on crime based on a nation's world system location, e.g., core, semi-periphery and periphery. This readily suggests the use of nested models in which variables from different theoretical perspectives serve as control for each other. It is also possible that interaction terms can be added to evaluate the specific impact of certain characteristics, e.g., political or economic systems.

If one is more interested in the nation specific effect, I suggest to add the dummy variables of those nations of interest into the regression equation to capture the differences in intercept. By carefully choosing a reference group, one can conveniently compare the specific effect of a particular nation to that of the reference group. In any circumstance, additional cultural, historical and legal background information are needed to explain the differences observed.

The Use of Diagnostic Tests

There are a few common methodological dilemmas in cross-national criminological research: (1) samples are not selected randomly; (2) sample size is often too small to provide enough degrees of freedom for significance tests and conclusions are vulnerable to the impact of a few influential cases; (3) only a limited number of variables can be included in the multivariate statistical analysis due to data availability problem; and (4) problems such as multicollinearity, heteroskedasticity, and autocorrelation make regression estimations less efficient. But, often times these problems are not detected nor treated. I argue that diagnostic tests are needed to better evaluate the data at hand and to help choose the proper statistical analytical tools.

From my initial examination of the descriptive statistics, I was able to describe variations in the means, standard deviations of the relevant variables as well as the number of available cases in this study. My examinations extended to include the comparison of descriptive statistics of the sub-sample groups. I also observed a severe problem of differential case attrition across different time periods. Because of the missing data problem observed in the descriptive statistics, I applied Heckman's procedure to diagnose the possible sample selection bias. I further tested for heteroskedasticity and offered proper solutions. Based on my diagnostic tests of possible outliers (or influential cases), my statistical models using cross-sectional data became significant when outliers were excluded.

Using a pooled cross-sectional time-series analysis technique, I am able to overcome some of the difficulties experienced in my cross-sectional analysis. I have a much larger sample size in the pooled data. I added control variables and included interaction terms. I divided my sample into different groups, e.g., developed and developing nations, or core and non-core nations and compared the results. I also assigned nation dummy variables to capture country specific effects on crime.

The methodological advantage of using pooled cross-sectional time-series analysis is obvious. I expect to see more usage of this technique in future cross-national studies. However, we are warned that the pooling methods may become a difficult exercise when the theoretical foundation of the regression model is weak (Sayrs, 1989). This reminds us of the reality that (1) comparative criminology is yet to become a matured and theoretically sophisticated field (Evans et al., 1996) and (2) we are still facing formidable methodological problems. For example, there are often too many missing values in one's data and a sample may not be normally distributed. Other arguments can be made on the definitions of crime variables and on the measurement of theoretical variables. This brings us to the discussion of the contributions and limitations of the study and my suggestions for future comparative research.

Contributions of the Study

There is a considerable amount of exchange between criminologists in the debate about theoretical elaboration versus theoretical integration as the proper strategy in developing explanations of crime. Some (e.g., Hirschi, 1989; Thornberry, 1989; Meier, 1989) suggest that criminological theories are underdeveloped and theoretical integration is premature. They recommend the strategy of theoretical elaboration-to fully develop existing theories. Others are more excited about exploring the potential of theoretical integration (e.g., Elliott, 1985; Elliott et al., 1985; Colvin and Pauly, 1983; Sampson, 1986). Theoretical integration, "an activity involving the formation of linkages among different theoretical arguments" (Liska et al., 1989:2; Wagner and Berger, 1985), is viewed as one way of theorizing to develop more forceful explanations and to promote theoretical growth.

In this study, I responded to the call for theory elaboration and integration by focusing on two comparative criminological theories-the Durkheimian and the Marxian perspectives. Efforts have been made to incorporate recent theoretical developments. The main focus of this study is theory elaboration, rather than integration. That is, I attempted to elaborate both the Durkheimian and Marxian perspectives by the logical extension of the basic propositions. For the elaborated Durkheimian perspective[11], I included both the concepts of "modernization" and "civilization". For the dynamic Marxian economic perspective, I included four dimensions: condition of capital, condition of labor, human investment and world system. For exploratory purposes, I also constructed a synthesized development model where I tested additional predictions (reflected by interaction terms) not directly made by the constituent theories-the Durkheimian and the Marxian perspectives. This synthesized developmental model is an exploratory attempt to theoretical integration.

Overall, I had at least moderate success in this study, judged by the empirical results. I hope I have succeeded in elaborating existing theories while reducing the number of propositions in the interest of parsimony. I also hope that my empirical findings, either confirmatory or contradictory to the hypotheses, will be helpful to future theory development.

From a methodological perspective, I took a systematic approach in dealing with several intricate and complex issues such as sample selection bias, influential cases and heteroskedasticity problems. Not only have I illustrated the utility of the pooled cross-sectional time-series analysis, I also demonstrated that the application of dual data structure (cross-sectional and pooled), multiple time periods (5 time periods in the cross-sectional data and 2 time periods in pooled data) and different analytical techniques (descriptive, bivariate, diagnostic and multivariate) result in robust findings with a high level of credibility. In short, I provided many constructive suggestions for solving the kind of problems one often encounters in comparative research.

Limitations of the Study

I have gained a good deal of first-hand knowledge about cross-national research from the current study. In fact, I suspect that some of the mixed findings are consequences of the methodological limitations of this study. First, sample composition may have caused some of the discrepancies in findings. Regression coefficients obtained from pooled analysis may be biased if the data base does not contain observations on comparable units. It is likely that both the estimations of regression coefficients and intercepts are swayed by the characteristics of nations that have more valid data points. Even if I am able to use nation dummy variables to capture country-specific effect, this procedure only changes the intercepts but not the slopes.

Second, I created two world system status dummy variables, SEMIPERI and PERIPH, based on Snyder and Kick's (1979) classifications. I did not investigate whether the status of a nation as either core, semi-periphery or periphery had changed in a time span of twenty-five years. Bollen (1983) argues that some countries are misclassified by Snyder and Kick (1979). For example, Bollen (1983) suggests that Spain and Portugal should be classified as semi-periphery nations not as core nations in the mid sixties.

Third, the measurement of moral individualism (MORAL) as the sum of political and civil rights was not available before 1973. I had to use democracy (DEMOC) as an approximate variable for moral individualism in analyses involving earlier time periods. Although MORAL and DEMOC are highly correlated in the time periods when both are available, I run the risk of assuming an equally high correlation in the earlier period which may or may not be justifiable.

Finally, the major limitation of the current study may be found in the problems inherent in the use of secondary, macro-level data for cross-national comparative purposes. I realize that, no matter how carefully I deal with data-related problems, the nature of the data used remain a major obstacle (see in He and Marshall, 1997).

Suggestions for Future Research

I suggest the following for future research. First, the Durkheimian and the Marxian perspectives remain valuable to comparative criminology, but further theory elaboration and integration are sorely needed. I need to work on constructing crime-specific hypotheses. I have found that the civilization dimension of the elaborated Durkheimian perspective adds strength to the traditional modernization perspective.

I suggest both concepts of civilization and modernization be included in future theorizing and testing of the Durkheimian approach.

For the Marxian perspective, the negative effect of surplus value on theft should be re-examined in different sample and in different time periods. The observed positive effect of government expenditure on human welfare on homicide is suggestive of a new hypothesis based on the concept of 'relative deprivation'. When 'relative deprivation' is defined as the excess of expectation over opportunities, Lea and Yong (1984) suggest that by providing minimum standards of living the modern Welfare State may also have raised minimum expectations. Crime could occur when expectations exceed the opportunities provided.

Second, comparative criminologists should seriously consider the advantages of using pooled cross-sectional time-series analysis. Cross-sectional regression analysis is sensitive to sample selection bias, missing value problem in the independent variables, multicollinearity problem and influential cases. I find diagnostic tests helpful in selecting appropriate analytical strategies. Cross-sectional analysis and pooled analysis can be complimentary to each other if proper care is taken.

Third, nation specific effects observed from my Least Square Dummy Variable (LSDV) analysis can be used to identify the countries of interest, e.g., those that appear to be "abnormal", for qualitative studies. For example, one might be interested in discovering (1) why as developed nations, the United States, Italy and France had homicide rates higher than the average of the developing nations in the 1960-1974 period; and (2) why other developed nations that shared the same characteristics did not? In the LSDV analysis, the nation dummy variables are only meaningful when additional background information, e.g., historical, economic, political and legal information, are acquired.

Lastly, I see a bright future for comparative criminology. There is now a surge of interest in conducting cross-national criminological research. International crime data are now available from more countries and for longer time periods.

Attempts at theory extrapolation and integration are promising. More sophisticated strategies for methodological improvement are also developing. I suggest that both the Durkheimian and the Marxian perspectives are valuable. Continuing to elaborate and integrate these two theoretical perspectives provides a worthwhile avenue for improving our understanding of macro-level crime in a comparative context.

Appendix I

* The World System Location measurement comes from

Snyder, David and Edward L. Kick (1979), Structural Position in the World System and Economic Growth, 1955-1970: A Multiple-Network Analysis of Transnational Interactions. American Journal of Sociology 84:1096-1126.

List of Core Nations (20 nations):

Canada, United States, United Kingdom, Netherlands, Belgium, Luxembourg, France, Switzerland, Spain, Portugal, West Germany, Austria, Italy, Yugoslavia, Greece, Sweden, Norway, Denmark, South Africa, Japan, Australia.

List of Semi-periphery Nations (29 nations):

Venezuela, Peru, Argentina, Uruguay, South Korea, Cuba, Ireland, East Germany, Hungary, Cyprus, Bulgaria, Rumania, U.S.S.R., Kenya, Iran, Turkey, Iraq, Lebanon, Jordan, Israel, Finland, Saudi Arabia, Taiwan, India, Pakistan, Burrna, Ceylon, Malaysia, Philippines.

List of Periphery Nations (61 nations):

Chad, Longo, Burundi, Rwanda, Somalia, Ethiopia, Malagasy Republic, Morocco, Algeria, Tunisia, Libya, Sudan, United Arab Republic, Yemen, Mali, Mauritania, Ghana, Upper Volta, Senegal, Dahomey, Nigeria, Cameroon, Niger, Gabon, Central African Republic, Panama, Colombia, Ecuador, Brazil, Bolivia, Paraguay, Chile. North Vietnam, Haiti, Dominican Republic, Mexico, Guatemala, Honduras, El Salvador, Nicaragua, Costa Rica, Jamaica, Trinidad and Tobago, Poland, Czechoslovakia, Malta, China (Peoples' Republic), Mongolian Republic, Nepal, Thailand, Cambodia, Laos, New Zealand, Iceland, Albania, Syria, Kuwait, Afghanistan, North Korea, South Vietnam, Indonesia.

* Moral Individualism (MORAL) is measured by using the sum of civil rights and political rights rating scores. The civil and political rights ratings for the time period of 1973 to 1984 are provided in:

> Gastil, Raymond Duncan (1990), The Comparative Survey of Freedom: Experiences and Suggestions. Studies in Comparative International Development 25:25-50.

Checklist for Civil Rights (Gastil, 1990:36-37):

1. Media/literature free of political censorship
      a. Press independent of government
      b. Broadcasting independent of government
2. Open public discussion
3. Freedom of assembly and demonstration
4. Freedom of political or quasi-political organization
5. Nondiscriminatory rule of law in political relevant cases
      a. Independent judiciary
      b. Security forces respect individuals
6. Free from unjustified political terror or imprisonment
      a. Free from imprisonment or exile for reasons of conscience
      b. Free from torture
      c. Free from terror by groups not opposed to the system
      d. Free from government-organized terror
7. Free trade unions, peasant organizations, or equivalents
g. Free businesses or cooperatives
9. Free professional or other private organizations
10. Free religious institutions
11. Personal social rights: including those to property, internal and external travel, choice of residence, marriage and family.
12. Socioeconomic rights: including freedom from dependency on landlords, bosses, union leaders, or bureaucrats
13. Freedom from gross socioeconomic inequality
14. Freedom from gross government indifference or corruption

Checklist for Political Rights (Gastil, 1990: 30-31):

1. Chief authority recently elected by a meaningful process
2. Legislature recently elected by a meaningful process

Alternatives for 1 and 2

a. No choice and possibility of rejection
b. No choice but some possibility of rejection
c. Government or single-party selected candidates
d. Choice possibly only among government-approved candidates
e. Relatively open choices possible only in local elections
f. Open choice possible within a restricted range
g. Relative open choices possible in all elections

3. Fair election laws, campaigning opportunity, polling and tabulation
4. Fair reflection of voter preference in distribution of power
5. Multiple political parties
    - only dominant party allowed effective opportunity
    - open to rise and fall of competing elections
6. Recent shifts in power through elections
7. Significant opposition vote
8. Free of military or foreign control
9. Major group or groups denied reasonable self-determination
10. Decentralized political power
11. Informal consensus; de facto opposition power.

The Rating System (Gastil, 1990: 28-29):

- Political Rights: Seven-point scale (1-7) - Civil Rights: Seven-point scale (1-7) - The freest rating is one and least free is seven.

* Democracy (DEMOC) is used as an approximate variable for Moral Individualism (MORAL) for the time period of 1960 to 1974. Data come from:

> Jaggers, Keith and Ted Robert Gurr (] 996), Polity III: Regime Change and Political Authority, 1800- 1994 [computer file]. Second ICPSR version. Boulder, CO: Keith Jagger/College Park, MD: Ted Robert Gurr [producers], 1995. Ann Arbor, Ml: Inter-university Consortium for Political and Social Research [distributor], 1996.

Variable DEMOC uses a 11 -point scale: 0 = low democracy; 10 = high democracy

* In the time period (1975-1984) when both measurements are available, variables MORAL and DEMOC are highly correlated. The correlation r equals to .93 and it is statistically significant at the .05 level.

Endnotes

1. Gastil's (1990) rating systems include a seven-point scale for both the civil rights and political rights measurement. Originally, they are used to construct freedom index in which the freest rating is one and least free is seven. I reversely coded both the civil and political rights so that one represent the least amount of rights and seven the most. Moral individualism measurement uses the summation scores of civil and political rights. Therefore, the values in the variable "moral individualism" now range from 2 (the lowest) to 14 (the highest).

2. Measurement for moral individualism was not available for the first pooled time period (1960-1974). I use "democracy " as a substitute measure for moral individualism in that time period. Democracy has a high correlation ($r = .93$) with moral individualism measured during the 1975-1984 time period when both data are available.

3. I suspect that a sample nation which has higher probability of missing crime data may also have greater contribution to the measurement error. Therefore, it is reasonable for one to check whether such a factor has contributed to the variance of error term in regression.

4. In both Table 8 and Table 9, the logistic models for the first three cross-sectional time periods: 1960-1964, 1965-1969 and 1970-1975 are not significant, except the 1970-1974 model which was used to predict missing homicide statistics using variables from the Durkheimian perspective. All other models using the cross-sectional data in the two later time periods: 1975-1979 and 1980-1984 are significant. And, all logistic models using the pooled data are significant.

5. According to Park's test procedure, base line regression equations are run first to obtain the residuals. Saved residuals are then squared and log transformed.

6. In particular, my procedure takes out the most severe outlier first, adds to it the next outlier until the statistical model can perform normally. I conducted initial test by running regression analyses without checking and taking out outlier. The initial results indicate poor fit of the statistical models.

7. When running the regression model including the hazard rate instrument variable, I detected severe multicollinearity problem. The hazard rate variable, being the saved predicted probability of missing crime statistics estimated in previous logistic regressions, is highly correlated to one or a few explanatory variables in the substantive regression equation. I use residualization technique (Roncek, 1997) to treat the collinearity problem. For example, if I find that an explanatory variable is highly correlated with the hazard rate variable, I would first regress this explanatory

variable on the hazard rate variable. I then save the residual from this bivariate regression. I use this residual rather than the original explanatory variable in the later regression analysis including the hazard rate variable. I expect that this residualization procedure will cure the collinearity problem. In fact, I argue that the use of this residual variable is justifiable. Because the common variance that an explanatory variable shares with the hazard variable has to be taken out before that variable can be used to predict the dependent variable.

8. Notice that the absolute values of the standardized regression coefficients (β) for the hazard rate variables in both equations in table 17 are greater than 1. This indicates that some collinearity problem still remains even after residualization procedure was performed. I suspect that this is due to the collinearity among more than two variables. Residualization technique may not be as effective in removing common variances in this situation. Ridge regression technique may be used to provide a solution.

9. The only exception is that the effect of government expenditure (GOVEXP) on theft in the 1975-1984 period was not statistically significant in table 23 but it is in table 24. However, the small differences in the unstandardized regression coefficients (.013 in OLS compared to .014 in WLS) and the identical standard errors (.007 in both) suggest that this observed change is insignificant.

10. The intercept in a regression model including nation dummy variables is actually the average score of the omitted group on the dependent variable. By running least square dummy variable regression model (LSDV), I would have single slope (one unstandardized coefficient for each independent variable) but multiple intercepts representing each of the specific nations under investigation. In table 25, for example, the true intercept for USA in the Durkheimian model on homicide (1960-1974) is 2.567 which is the sum of the intercept of the regression model, i.e., 1.732 and the USA specific coefficient, i.e., .835. Likewise, in the same regression model the true intercept for Canada is 1.143 which is the sum of the intercept of the regression model, i.e., 1.732 and the Canada specific coefficient, i.e., -.589. Thus, if I am to plot regression lines for each developed nations listed in table 25, I would see parallel straight lines taking off from different points on the Y axis.

Bibliography

Akers, Ronald L.
  1979 Theory and Ideology in Marxist Criminology. Criminology 16:527-544.
  1980 Further Critical Thoughts on Marxist Criminology: Comment on Turk, Toby, and Klockars. In James A Inciardi (ed.), Radical Criminology: The Coming Crises, pp. 133-138. Beverly Hills, CA:Sage.
  1997 Criminological Theories: Introduction and Evaluation (2nd ed.). Los Angeles, CA: Roxbury Publishing Co.

Amsden, Alice H.
  1981 An International Comparison of the Rate of Surplus Value in Manufacturing Industry. Cambridge Journal of Economics 5:229-249.

Archer, Dane and Rosemary Gartner
  1984 Violence and Crime in Cross-National Perspective. New Haven, CT: Yale University Press.

Avison William R. and Pamela L. Loring
  1986 Population Diversity and Cross-National Homicide; The Effects of Inequality and Heterogeneity. Criminology 24:733-749.

Balbus, Isaac D.
  1977 Commodity Form and Legal Form: An Essay on the 'relative autonomy' of the State. Law and Society Review 11:571-588.

Barberet, Rosemary Louise
  1994 Modernization, Criminal Sanctions and Crime in Spain, 1960-1989. Ph.D. Dissertation, College Park: University of Maryland.

Barlow, David E. and W. Wesley Johnson
  1996 The Political Economy of Criminal Justice Policy: A Time-Series Analysis of Economic Conditions, Crime, and Federal Criminal Justice Legislation, 1948-1987. Justice Quarterly 13:223-241.

Barnett, Harold
  1981 Wealth, Crime and Capital Accumulation. In Greenberg (ed.), Crime and Capitalism. Palo Alto, CA: Mayfield.

Beirne, Piers
  1979 Empiricism and the Critique of Marxism on Law and Crime. Social Problems 26:373-385.
  1983 Cultural Relativism and Comparative Criminology. Contemporary Crises 7:371-391.

Beirne, Piers and James Messerschmidt
1995 Criminology. San Diego: Harcourt Brace Jovanovich.

Bennett, Richard R.
1991 Development and Crime: A Cross-National, Time-Series Analysis of Competing Models. The Sociological Quarterly 32:343-363.
1992 Correlates of Crime: A Study of 52 Nations, 1960-1984[computer file]. Washington, D.C.: Richard R. Bennett, The American University[producer], 1987. Ann Arbor, MI: Inter-university Consortium for Political and Social Research[distributor], 1992.

Bennett, Richard and Peter Bostiotis
1991 Structural Correlates of Juvenile Property Crime: A Cross-National Time-Series Analysis. Journal of Research in Crime and Delinquency 28:262-287.

Berk, Richard A.
1983 An Introduction to Sample Selection Bias in Sociological Data. American Sociological Review 48:386-398.

Birkbeck, C.
1985 Understanding Crime and Social Control Elsewhere: A Geographic Perspective on Theory in Criminology. Research in Law, Deviance and Social Control 7:215-246.

Blazicek, D and G. M. Janeksela
1978 Some Comments on Comparative Methodologies in Criminal Justice. International Journal of Criminology and Penology 6:233-245.

Block, Fred
1977 The Ruling Class Does Not Rule. Socialist Revolution 33:23.
1981 Beyond Relative Autonomy: State Managers as Historical Subjects. New Political Science 2:39.

Block, Alan A. and William J. Chambliss
1981 Organizing Crime. New York: Elsevier.

Blumstein, Alfred and Jacqueline Cohen
1973 A Theory of the Stability of Punishment. Journal of Criminal Law and Criminology 64:198-207.

Bollen, Kenneth A.
1983 World System Position, Dependency and Democracy. American Sociological Review 48:468-79.

Bonger, W.
   1969[1916]   Criminality and Economic Conditions. Boston: Little, Brown and
                Company.

Bornschier V. and C. Chase-Dunn
   1985 Transnational Corporations and underdevelopment. New York: Praeger.

Bottomore, Tom (ed.)
   1991 A Dictionary of Marxist Thought (2nd ed.). Cambridge, MA: Blackwell
         Publishers.

Bottomore, Tom and Maximilien Rubel
   1961 Karl Marx: Selected Writings in Sociology and Social Philosophy. London.

Braithwaite, John and Valerie Braithwaite
   1980 The Effect of Income Inequality and Social Democracy on Homicide. British
         Journal of Criminology 20:45-53.

Briggs, C. M. and P. Cutright
   1994 Structural and Cultural Determinants of Child Homicide: A Cross-National
         Analysis. Violence and Victims 9:3-16.

Burgess, Ernest W.
   1928 The Growth of the City. In Park, Burgess and McKenzie, The City. Chicago:
         University of Chicago Press.

Bush, Rod
   1983 Racism and Changes in the International Division of Labor. Crime and
         Social Justice 20:37-49.

Campbell, Tom
   1981 Seven Theories of Human Society. Oxford, UK: Clarendon Press.

Chambliss, William J.
   1976 Functional and Conflict Theories of Crime. In William J. Chambliss and M.
         Mankoff (eds.), Whose Law? What Order? New York: John Wiley.
   1988 Exploring Criminology. New York, NY: Macmillan.

Chambliss, William J. and Robert B. Seidman
   1982 Law, Order, and Power. Second edition. Reading, MA: Adison-Wesley.

Chandler, Charles R.
  1984 Durkheim and Individualism: A Comment on Messner. Social Forces 63:571-573.

Chase-Dunn, Christopher
  1975 The Effects of International Economic Dependence on Development and Inequality. American Sociological Review 40:720-39.

Chase-Dunn, C. and R. Rubinson
  1979 Cycles, Trends, and New Departures in World-System Development. In J. Meyer and M. Hannah (eds.), National Development and the World System. Chicago: University of Chicago Press.

Chen, Danny J. H.
  1992 Third World Crime in the World System: A Cross-National Study. Ph. D. Dissertation, Albany, SUNY.

Clark, Roger
  1989 Cross-National Perspectives on Female Crime: An Empirical Investigation. International Journal of Comparative Sociology 30:195-215.

Clifford, W.
  1978 Culture and Crime in Global Perspective. International Journal of Criminology and Penology 6:61-80.

Clinard, Marshall B. and Daniel J. Abbott
  1973 Crime in Developing Countries: A Comparative Perspective. New York: John Wiley.

Cohen, Jacob and Patricia Cohen,
  1975 Applied Multiple Regression/Correlation Analysis for the Behavioral Sciences. New York: Halsted.

Cohen, Stanley
  1982 Western Crime Control Models in the Third World: Benign or Malignant? Research in Law, Deviance and Social Control 4:85-119.

Collette, John, Stephen D. Webb and David L. Smith
  1979 Suicide, Alcoholism and Types of Social Integration: Clarification of a Theoretical Legacy. Sociology and Social Research 63:699-721.

Colvin, M. and J. Pauly
  1983 A Critique of Criminology: Toward an Integrated Structural-Marxist Theory of Delinquency Production. American Journal of Sociology 90:513-551.

Conklin, George H. and Miles E. Simpson
  1985 A Demographic Approach to the Cross-National Study of Homicide. Comparative Social Research 8:171-185.

Cueno, Carl J.
  1978 Class Exploitation in Canada. Canadian Review of Sociology and Anthropology 15:284-300.
  1982 Class Struggle and Measure of the Rate of Surplus Value. Canadian Review of Sociology and Anthropology 19:377-425.
  1984 Reconfirming Karl Marx's Rate of Surplus Value. Canadian Review of Sociology and Anthropology 21:98-104.

DeFronzo, James
  1983 Economic Assistance to Impoverished Americans: Relationship to Incidence of Crime. Criminology 21:119-36.
  1996 Welfare and Burglary. Crime and Delinquency 42:223-30.
  1997 Welfare and Homicide. Journal of Research in Crime and Delinquency 34:395-406.

Denisoff, R. S. and D. McQuarie
  1975 Crime Control in Capitalist Society: A Reply to Quinney. Issues in Criminology 10:109-119.

Devine, J. A., J. F. Sheley and M. D. Smith
  1988 Macroeconomic and Social Control Policy Influences on Crime Rate Changes, 1948-1985. American Sociological Review 53:407-20.

Domhoff, G. William
  1979 The Powers That Be. New York: Vintage.
  1981 Provincial in Paris: Finding the French Council on Foreign Relations. Social Policy, March-April.

Donner, Allan
  1982 The Relative Effectiveness of Procedures Commonly Used in Multiple Regression Analysis for Dealing With Missing Values. The American Statistician 36:378-381.

196

Durkheim, Emile
  1933[1893] The Division of Labor in Society (trans. George Simpson). New York: Free Press.
  1950[1895] Les regles de la methode sociologique. Paris.
  1951[1897] Suicide. Translated by John A Spaulding and George Simpson. New York: Free Press.
  1964[1895] The Rules of Sociological Method. New York: Free Press.
  1964[1893] The Division of Labor in Society. New York: Free Press.
  1965[1912] The Elementary Forms of the Religious Life, translated by Joseph W. Swain. New York: Free Press.
  1973[1900] Two Laws of Penal Evolution. T. Anthony Jones and Andrew T. Scull (trs.). Economy and Society 2:285-308.
  1982[1902] Civilisation in General and Types of Civilisation. In Steven Lukes (ed.), Durkheim: The Rules of Sociological Method and Selected Texts on Sociology and its Method. pp. 243-244. New York: The Free Press.
  1982[1895] The Rules of Sociological Method. In Steven Lukes (ed.), The Sociological Method and Selected Texts on Sociology and Its Methods, pp. 31-163. New York: The Free Press.
  1984[1893] The Division of Labor in Society. Translated by W.D. Halls. New York: Free Press.

Einstadter, Werner and Stuart Henry
  1995 Criminological Theory: An Analysis of Its Underlying Assumptions. Ft. Worth: Harcourt Brace College Publishers.

Elias, Norbert
  1982 The Civilizing Process: The History of Manners and State Formation and Civilization (translated by Edmund Jephcott). Oxford, UK: Blackwell Publishers Ltd.

Elliott, Delbert
  1985 The Assumption That Theories Can Be Combined With Increased Explanatory. In Theoretical Methods in Criminology, edited by Robert F. Meier, pp.123-149. Beverly Hills, CA: Sage.

Elliott, Delbert, David Huzinga and Suzanne S. Ageton
  1985 Explaining Delinquency and Drug Use. Beverly Hills, CA: Sage.

Engels, Fredrick
  1964 [1844] Outlines of a Critique of Political Economy. In D. Struik, ed. The Economic and Philosophic Manuscripts of 1844. New York: International Publishers.

1973[1845] The Conditions of the Working Class in England. Moscow: Progress Publishers.
1978[1894] Anti-Durhing. Moscow: Progress Publishers.
1981   Demoralization of the English Working Class. In D. Greenberg, ed. Crime and Capitalism. Palo Alto, CA: Mayfield.
1983   Crisis, Joint-Stock Companies, and State Intervention. In Tom Bottomore and Patrick Goode (eds.), Readings in Marxist Sociology. Oxford: Clarendon Press.

Evans, T. David, Randy L. Lagrange and Cecil L. Willis
    1996 Theoretical Development of Comparative Criminology: Rekindling an Interest. International Journal of Comparative and Applied Criminal Justice 20:15-29.

Evans, Peter and Michael Timberlake
    1980 Dependence, Inequality, and the Growth of the Tertiary: A Comparative Analysis of Less Developed Countries. American Sociological Review 45:531-532.

Fiala, R. and G. LaFree
    1988 Cross-National Determinants of Child Homicide. American Sociological Review 53:432-45.

Friday, Paul
    1996 The Need to Integrate Comparative and International Criminal Justice into a Traditional Curriculum. Journal of Criminal Justice Education 7:227-239.

Friedrichs, David O.
    1979 The Law and the Legitimacy Crisis. In R. G. Iacovetta and Dae H. Chang(eds.),
        Critical Issues in Criminal Justice. Durham, N. C.: Carolina Press.

Gartner, R.
    1990 The Victims of Homicide: A Temporal and Cross-National Comparison. American Sociological Review 55:92-106.
    1991 Family Structure, Welfare Spending and Child Homicide in Developed Democracies. Journal of Marriage and the Family 53:231-40.

Giddens, Anthony
    1971 Capitalism and Modern Social Theory: An Analysis of the Writings of Marx, Durkheim and Max Weber. Cambridge, UK: Cambridge University Press.

198

Glaser, Daniel
1964 The Effectiveness of a Prison and Parole System, Indianapolis: Bobbs-Merrill.

Greenberg, David F.
1976 On One-Dimensional Criminology. Theory and Society 3: 610-21.

Greenberg, David F.
1980 Penal Sanctions in Poland: A Test of Alternative Models. Social Problems 28:194-204.
1981 Crime and Capitalism. Palo Alto, CA: Mayfield.

Groves, W. Byron and Nancy Frank
1987 Punishment and the Sociology of Structured Choice. In W. B. Groves and G.R. Newman (eds.), Punishment and Privilege. New York: Harrow and Heston.

Groves, W. Byron, Richard McClearly and Graeme R. Newman
1985 Religion, Modernization, and World Crime. Comparative Social Research 8:59-78.

Gunst, Richard F. and Robert L. Mason
1980 Regression Analysis and Its Application: A Data-Oriented Approach. New York: Marcel Dekker, Inc.

Gurr, Ted Robert
1989 Historical Trends in Violent Crime: Europe and the United States. In Ted R. Gurr (ed.), Violence in America, vol. 1: The History of Crime, pp. 21-54. Newbury Park, CA; Sage.

Gurr, Ted. R., P. Grabosky and R. Hula
1977 Politics of Crime and Conflict: A Comparative History of Four Cities. Beverly Hills, CA: Sage.

Hansmann, H. and J. Quigley
1982 Population Heterogeneity and the Sociogenesis of Homicide. Social Forces 61:106-224.

Hartnagal, Timonthy F.
1982 Modernization, Female Social Roles, and Female Crime: A Cross-National Investigation. Sociological Quarterly 23:477-490.

Hartnagal, Timothy and Muhammad Mizanuddin
1986 Modernization, Gender Role Convergence and Female Crime: A Further Test. International Journal of Comparative Sociology 27:1-14.

He, Ni and Ineke Haen Marshall
1997 Social Production of Crime Data: A Critical Examination of Chinese Crime Statistics. International Criminal Justice Review 7:46-64.

Henry, Stuart and Dragon Milovanovic
1996 Constitutive Criminology: Beyond Postmodernism. London, UK: Sage.

Hicks, Alexander M.
1994 Introduction to Pooling. In Thomas Janoski and Alexander M. Hicks (eds.), The Comparative Political Economy of the Welfare State, pp. 169-188. Cambridge, UK: Cambridge University Press.

Heiland, Hans-Gunther and Louise Shelley
1991 Civilization, Modernization and the Development of Crime and Control. In Hans-Gunther Heiland, Louise I. Shelley and Hisao Katoh (eds.), Crime and Control in Comparative Perspectives. Berlin, Germany: Walter de Gruyter & Co.

Hinch, Ronald
1983 Marxist Criminology in the 1970s: Clarifying the Clutter. Crime and Social Justice, summer:65-74.

Hirschi, Travis
1969 Causes of Delinquency. Berkeley, CA: University of California Press.
1989 Exploring Alternatives to Integrated Theory. In Messner, Krohn and Liska (eds.), Theoretical Integration in the Study of Deviance and Crime, pp. 37-50. Albany, NY: SUNY Press.

Hirst, Paul Q.
1972 Marx and Engels on Crime, Law and Morality. Economy and Society 1:28-56.
1975 Radical Deviancy Theory and Marxism: A Reply to Taylor and Walton. In Taylor, Walton, and Young (eds.), Critical Criminology. Boston, MA: Routledge and Kegan Paul.
1979 On Law and Ideology. Atlantic Fields, NJ: Humanity Press.

Horton, John and Tony Platt
1986 Crime and Criminal Justice Under Capitalism and Socialism: Toward a Marxist Perspective. Crime and Social Justice 25:115-135.

200

Huang, Wei-Sung Wilson
1995 A Cross-National Analysis on the Effect of Moral Individualism on Murder Rates. International Journal of Offender Therapy and Comparative Criminology 39:63-75.

Huggins, Martha Knisely
1985 Approaches to Crime and Societal Development. Comparative Social Research 8: 17-35.

Humphries, Drew and Don Wallace,
1980 Capitalist Accumulation and Urban Crime, 1950-1971. Social Problems 28:179-193.

Jaggers, Keith and Ted R. Gurr
1996 Polity III: Regime Type and Political Authority, 1800-1994. [computer file]. 2nd ICPSR version. Boulder, CO:Keith Jaggers/College Park, MD: Ted Robert Gurr[producers], 1995. Ann Arbor, MI: Inter-university Consortium for Political and Social Research[distributor], 1996.

Jensen, Gary F.
1980 Labeling and Identity: Toward a Reconciliation of Divergent Findings. Criminology 18:121-129.

Jessop, Bob
1982 The Capitalist State. Oxford: Martin Robertson.

Jones, T. Anthony
1981 Durkheim, Deviance and Development: Opportunities Lost and Regained. Social Forces 59:1009-1024.

Judge, George, W.D. Griffith, R. C. Hill, H. Lutkepohl, and T. C. Lee
1988 The Theory and Practice of Econometrics. 2nd ed. New York: Wiley.

Kasinitz, Philip
1983 Neo-Marxist Views of the State. Dissent 30:337-346.

Kellogg, Frederic R.
1977 Criminal Penalties and Social Evolution: Durkheimian Perspectives. Annee-Sociologique 28:79-93.

Kick, Edward L. and Gary D. LaFree
1985 Development and Social Context of Murder and Theft. Comparative Social Research 8:37-57.

Kim, Sung-Soon-Clara, Burke D. Grandjean and M. Milner
1993 Solidarity and Deviance: Durkheimian Source of Solidarity in American Cities. Sociological Abstracts, Inc.

Klockars, Carl
1980 The Contemporary Crisis of Marxist Criminology. In James Inciardi (ed.), Radical Criminology. Beverly Hills, CA: Sage.

Kmenta, Jan
1988[1971] Elements of Econometrics. New York: Macmillan.

Koppel, David B.
1992 The Samurai, the Mountie and the Cowboy: Should American Adopt the Gun Controls of Other Democracies? Buffalo, NY: Prometheus Books.

Korsch, Karl
1967[1938] Karl Marx. London: Chapman & Hall.

Krahn, H., T. Hartnagel, and J. Gartrel
1986 Income Inequality and Homicide Rates: Cross-National Data and Criminological Theories. Criminology 24:269-295.

Krohn, Marvin D.
1976 Inequality, Unemployment and Crime: A Cross-National Analysis. Sociological Quarterly 17:303-313.

Krohn, M. and C. Wellford
1977 A Static and Dynamic Analysis of Crime and the Primary Dimensions of Nations. International Journal of Criminology and Penology 5:1-16.

Krohn, Marvin D.
1978 A Durkheimian Analysis of International Crime Rates. Social Forces 57:654-670.

LaFree, Gary
1997 Comparative Cross-National Studies of Homicide. In Dwayne Smith and Margaret Zahn(eds.), Homicide Studies: A Sourcebook of Social Research. Sage.

LaFree, Gary and Edward L. Kick
1986 Cross-National Effects of Developmental, Distributional, and Demographic Variables on Crime: A Review and Analysis. International Annals of Criminology 24:213-236.

Lea, John and Jock Young
1984 What is to be Done about Law and Order? Harmondsworth: Penguin.

Leavitt, Gregory C.
1992 General Evolution and Durkheim's Hypothesis of Crime Frequency: A Cross-Cultural Test. Sociological Quarterly 33:241-263.

Lester, David
1987 Why People Kill Themselves. Springfield, IL: Charles C. Thomas.

Levy, Marion
1966 Modernization and the Structure of Societies. Princeton: Princeton University Press.

Liska, Allen E., Marvin D. Krohn and Steven Messner
1989 Strategies and Requisites for Theoretical Integration in the Study of Crime and Deviance. In Messner, Krohn and Liska (eds.), Theoretical Integration in the Study of Deviance and Crime, pp. 1-20. Albany, NY: SUNY Press.

Little, R. and D. Robin
1987 Statistical Analysis with Missing Data. New York: Wiley.

Lodhi, A. Q. and C. Tilly
1973 Urbanization, Crime and Collective Violence in Nineteenth Century France. American Journal of Sociology 79:297-318.

Lopez-Ray, M.
1970 Crime: An Analytical Appraisal. London: Routledge & Kegan Paul.

Lukic, Radomir D.
1974 The Functionalist Conception of the Social Basis of Morality. Sociologija 16:169-193.

Lynch, James P.
1995 Building Data System for Cross-National Comparisons of Crime and Criminal Justice Policy: A Retrospective. ICPSR Bulletin 15:1-6.

Lynch, Michael J.
1987 Quantitative Analysis and Marxist Criminology. Crime and Social Justice 29:110-127.

Lynch, Michael J. and W. Byron Grove
1986 A Primer in Radical Criminology. Albany, NY: Harrow and Heston.

1989 A Primer in Radical Criminology. Second Edition. New York: Harrow and Heston.

Lynch, Michael J., Byron W. Groves and Alan Lizotte
1994 The Rate of Surplus Value and Crime: A Theoretical and Empirical Examination of Marxian Economic Theory and Criminology. Crime, Law and Social Change 21:15-48.

Lynch, M. J., G. R. Newman, D. McDowall and W. B. Groves
1988 Crime in the World System: An Introduction to World System Theory and Its Implications for Comparative Criminology. Paper Presented at the Meeting of the American Society of Criminology, Chicago, IL.

Machalek, Richard and Lawrence E. Cohen
1991 An Evolutionary Emendation of Durkheim's theory of Crime. Unpublished paper.

Maddala, G .S.
1971 The Use of Variance Components Models in Pooling Cross Section and Time Series Data. Econometrica 39:341-358.

Marx, Karl
1974 Capital, Volume I. New York: New World Paperbacks.
1981 Capital, Volume III. New York: International.
1981 Crime and Capital Accumulation. In David Greenberg (ed.), Crime and Capitalism. Palo Alto, CA; Mayfield.
1982[1847] The Poverty of Philosophy. New York: International Publishers.
1982[1859] A Contribution to the Critique of Political Economy. New York, NY: International Publishers.

Marx, Karl and Fredrick Engels,
1965 The German Ideology. London: Lawrence and Wishart.

Matza, David
1964 Delinquency and Drift. New York: Wiley.

Maurer, Michael
1991 American Behind Bars; A Comparison of International Rates of Incarceration. Washington D.C.: The Sentencing Project.

McDonald, Lynn
1976 The Sociology of Law and Order. Boulder, CO: Westview Press.

Meier, Robert F.
1989 Deviance and Differentiation.   In Messner, Krohn and Liska (eds.), Theoretical Integration in the Study of Deviance and Crime, pp. 199-212. Albany, NY: SUNY Press.

Merton, Robert K.
1938 Social Structure and Anomie. American Sociological Review 3:672-682.

Messner, Steven F.
1982 Societal Development, Social Equality, and Homicide: A Cross-National Test of a Durkheimian Model. Social Forces 61:225-240.
1992 Exploring the Consequences of Erratic Data Reporting for Cross-National Research on Homicide. Journal of Quantitative Criminology 8:155-173.

Messner, Steven F. and Richard Rosenfeld
1994 Crime and the American Dream. Belmont, CA: Wadsworth Publishing Company.
1997 Crime and the American Dream. Second Edition. Belmont, CA: Wadworth Publishing Company.

Mestrovic, Stjepan C. and Geoffrey P. Alpert
1989 The Stock Market Crash of 1987 and Durkheim's Concept of Economic Anomie: Shifting the Focus of Anomie Research From Crime to Business. Unpublished Paper.

Muller, Edward N.
1986 Income Inequality and Political Violence; The Effects of Influential Cases. American Sociological Review 51:441-445.

Mungham, G.
1980 The Career of a Confusion: Radical Criminology in Britain. In J. Inciardi (ed.), Radical Criminology: The Coming Crisis. Beverly Hills, CA: Sage.

Nelson, F.
1984 Efficiency of the Two-Step Estimator for Models with Endogenous Sample Selection. Journal of Econometrics 24:181-196.

Neuman, Lawrence W. and Ronald J. Berger
1988 Competing Perspectives on Cross-National Crime: An Evaluation of Theory and Evidence. Sociological Quarterly 29:281-313.

Newman, Graeme
1976 Comparative Deviance. New York: Elsevier.

Nye, F. Ian
1958 Family Relationships and Delinquent Behavior. New York: Wiley.

Ortega, Suzanne T., Jay Corzine, Cathleen Burnett and Tracey Poyer
1992 Modernization, Age Structure, and Regional Context: A Cross-National Study of Crime. Sociological Spectrum 12:257-277.

Paarsch, H.
1984 A Monte Carlo Comparison of Estimators for Censored Regression Models. Journal of Econometrics 24:197-213.

Pampel, F. C. and R. Gartner
1995 Age Structure , Socio-Political Institutions, and National Homicide Rates. European Sociological Review 11:243-60.

Park, Robert, E.
1936 Human Ecology. American Journal of Sociology 42:158.

Poulantzas, Nicos
1969 The Problem of the Capitalist State. New Left Review 58: 67-78.
1973 Political Power and Social Classes. London: Verso.

Quinney, Richard
1970 The Social Reality of Crime. Boston: Little, Brown.
1980 Class, State and Crime. New York: Longman.

Reckless, Walter
1961 A New Theory of Delinquency and Crime. Federal Probation 25:42-46.

Reiss, Albert J.
1951 Delinquency as the Failure of Personal and Social Controls. American Sociological Review 16:196-207.

Robertson, Roland
1992 Globalization: Social Theory and Global Culture. Newbury Park, CA: Sage.

Rogers, John D.
1989 Theories of Crime and Development: An Historical Perspective. Journal of Development Studies 25:314-328.

Roncek, Dennis W.
1996 A Simpler Procedure for Avoiding Multicollinearity Problems in Identifying Interaction Effects. Paper Presented at the 1996 Annual Meetings of the

206

American Society of Criminology in Chicago, IL.

1997 A Regression-Based Strategy for Coping with Multicollinearity. Paper presented at the 1997 Annual Meetings of the Midwest Sociological Society in Des Moines, Iowa.

Roshier, Bob
1977 The Function of Crime Myth. Sociological Review 25:309-324.

Sampson, Robert J.
1986 Effects of Socioeconomic Context on Official Reaction to Juvenile Delinquency. American Sociological Review 49:261-272.

Sayrs, Lois W.
1989 Pooled Time Series Analysis. Newbury Park, CA: Sage Publications, Inc.

Schattenberg, Gus
1981 Social Control Functions of Mass Media Depictions of Crime. Sociological Inquiry 51:71-77.

Schwendinger, Julia R. and Herman Schwendinger,
1985 Adolescent Subcultures and Delinquency. New York: Praeger.

Shaw, Clifford and Henry D. McKay
1931 Social Factors in Juvenile Delinquency: A Study of the Community, the Family and the Gang in Relation to Delinquent Behavior, National Commission on Law Observance and Enforcement: Report on the Causes of Crime Vol. II, Washington: US Government Printing Office.
1942 Juvenile Delinquency and Urban Areas. Chicago: University of Chicago Press.

Shelley, Louise I.
1985 American Crime: An International Anomaly? Comparative Social Research 8:81-96.

Shichor, David
1980 The New Criminology: Some Critical Issues. British Journal of Criminology 20:1-19.
1985 Effects of Development on Official Crime Rates 1967-1978: Homicide and Larceny Patterns Differ Greatly. Sociology and Social Research 70:96-97.

Simcha-Facan, O. and J. E. Schwartz
1986 Neighborhood and Delinquency: An Assessment of Contextual Effects. Criminology 24:667-703.

Simpson, Miles E. and George H. Conklin
1992 Homicide, Inequality, Political Systems and Transnational Corporation: A Cross-National Study. Sociological Abstracts, Inc.

Sims, Barbara A.
1997 Crime, Punishment, and the American Dream: Toward a Marxist Integration. Journal of Research in Crime and Delinquency 34:5-24.

Smith, Kent W. and M. S. Sasaki
1979 Decreasing Multicollinearity: A Method for Models with Multiplicative Functions. Sociological Methods & Research 8:35-56.

Smith, Earl and Wong Siu-Kwong
1989 Durkheim, Individualism and Homicide Rates Re-Examined. Sociological Spectrum 9:269-283.

Sparks, R. F.
1980 A Critique of Marxist Criminology. In N. Morris and M. Tonry (eds.), Crime and Justice: An Annual Review of Research. Chicago: University of Chicago Press.

Spitzer, Steven
1975 Toward a Marxian Theory of Deviance. Social Problems 22:638-651.
1980 Toward a Marxian Theory of Deviance. In D. Kelly (ed.), Criminal Behavior. New York: St. Martins.

Stack, Steven
1978 Suicide: A Comparative Analysis. Social Forces 57:630-653(??).
1984 Income Inequality and Property Crime. Criminology 22:229-258.

Stimson, James A.
1985 Regression in Time and Space: A Statistical Essay. American Journal of Political Science 29:915-947.

Stolzenberg, Ross, M. and Daniel A. Relles
1990 Theory Testing in a World of Constrained Research Design: The Significance of Heckman's Censored Sampling Bias Correction for Nonexperimental Research. Sociological Methods and Research 18:395-415.

Studenmund, A. H.
1992 Using Econometrics: A Practical Guide (2nd ed.). New York, NY: HarperCollins Publishers.

Sumner, Colin
1982 Crime, justice and Underdevelopment. London: Macmillan.

Sykes, G.
1974 The Rise of Critical Criminology. Journal of Criminal Law and Criminology 65:206-213.

Szabo, D.
1975 Comparative Criminology. Journal of Criminal Law and Criminology 66:366-379.

Takala, Jukka-Pekka
1992 The Necessity and Utility of Crime: Roots of a Strange Way of Speaking. Sosiologia 29:73-88.

Taylor, William E.
1980 Small Sample Considerations in Estimations in Estimations from Panel Data. Journal of Econometrics 13:203-223.

Taylor, Ian, Paul Walton and Jock Young
1973 The New Criminology: For a Social Theory of Deviance. New York: Harper and Row.
1975 Critical Criminology. London: Routledge and Kegan Paul.

Thornberry, Terrence P.
1989 Exploring Alternatives to Integrated Theory. In Messner, Krohn and Liska (eds.), Theoretical Integration in the Study of Deviance and Crime, pp. 50-60. Albany, NY: SUNY Press.

Toby, Jackson
1957 Social Disorganization and Stake in Conformity: Complementary Factors in the Predatory Behavior of Hoodlums. Journal of Criminal Law, Criminology, and Police Science 48:12-17.

Trebach, Arnold S. and James A. Inciardi
1993 Legalize It? Debating American Drug Policy. Washington, D.C.: American University Press.

United Nations
1986 Handbook of National Accounting. Accounting for Production: Sources and Methods.

United Nations
1983 Questionnaires: The Second United Nations Survey of Crime Trends, Operations of Criminal Justice Systems and Crime Prevention Strategies. Vienna, Austria: Crime Prevention and Criminal Justice Branch Center for Social Development and Humanitarian Affairs, United Nations.
1988 Questionnaires: The Third United Nations Survey of Crime Trends, Operations of Criminal Justice Systems and Crime Prevention Strategies. Vienna, Austria: Crime Prevention and Criminal Justice Brance Center for Social Development and Humanitarian Affairs, United Nations.

Unnithan, N. Prabha, Lin Huff-Corzine, Jay Corzine and Hugh P. Whitt
1994 The Currents of Lethal Violence: An Integrated Model of Suicide and Homicide. Albany, NY: SUNY Press.

Unnithan, Prabha N. and Hugh P. Whitt
1992 Inequality, Economic Development and Lethal Violence: A Cross-National Analysis of Suicide and Homicide. International Journal of Comparative Sociology 33:182-196.

Van Dijk, Jan J.M.
1989 Penal Sanctions and the Process of Civilization. In Annales internationales de Criminologie 27:191-204.

Vold, George B. and Thomas J. Bernard
1986 Theoretical Criminology (3rd ed.). New York: Oxford University Press.

Wagner, David and Joseph Berger
1985 Do Sociological Theory Grow? American Journal of Sociology 90:697-728.

Wallace, D. and D. Humphries
1981 Urban Crime and Capitalist Accumulation:1950-1971. In D. Greenberg (ed.), Crime and Capitalism. Polo Alto, CA: Mayfield.

Wallerstein, I.
1974 The Modern World System: Capitalist Agriculture and the Origins of the European World Economy in the Sixteenth Century. New York; Academic Press.
1991 The National and the Universal: Can There Be Such a Thing as World Culture? In A. D. King (ed.), Culture, Globalization and the World-System.

Walton, J.
1982 The International Economy and Periphery Urbanization. In N. I. Fainstein and S. S. Fainstein (eds.), Urban Policy Under Capitalism, pp. 119-315.

Beverly Hills, CA: Sage.

Weber, Alfred
1920 Prinzipielles zur Kultursoziologie: Gesellschafts-prozess, Zivilisationsprozess und Kulturbewegung. In Archiv fur Sozialwissenschaft und Sozialpolitik 47:1-49.

Weede, Erich
1986 Income Inequality and Political Violence Reconsidered. American Sociological Review 51:438-441.

Weisberg, Sanford
1980 Applied Linear Regression. New York: Wiley.

Wellford, Charles F.
1974 Crime and the Dimensions of Nations. International Journal of Criminology and Penology 2:1-10.

White, H.
1980 A Heteroskedasticity-Consistent Covariance Matrix and A Direct Test for Heteroscedasticity. Econometrica 48:817-838.

Wilks, S. S.
1932 Certain Generalizations in the Analysis of Variance. Biometrika 24:471-494.

Wolf, Preben
1971 Crime and Development: An International Comparison of Crime Rates. Scandinavian Studies in Criminology 3;107-120.

Zehr, Howard
1976 Crime and the Development of Modern Society: Pattern of Criminality in 19th Century Germany and France, Rowman and Littlefield.

218

156
vector, 71, 72
vice, 7, 43, 49, 53
violent crime, 12, 29, 34, 38, 53, 64,
          142, 165, 167
Vold, George B., 153
W.D. Griffith, 144
W. B. Groves, 142, 147
W. Byron Grove, 146
W. Wesley Johnson, 135
Wagner, David, 153
Wallace, D., 153
Wallerstein, I., 153
Walton, J., 153
Weber, Alfred, 154
Weede, Erich, 154
weighted least square (WLS), 23, 27,
          67, 105
weighting procedure, 67
weights, 67
Weisberg, Sanford, 154
welfare, 9, 13, 25, 33, 51, 54, 61, 62,
          65, 86, 139, 141, 143,
          166, 167, 171, 175,
          183
welfare state, 13, 33, 143, 183
Wellford, Charles F., 154
Western democracies, 20
White, H., 154
white-collar crime, 29
Wilks, S. S., 154
William J. Chambliss, 136, 137
Wolf, Preben, 154
Wong Siu-Kwong, 151
working class, 8, 9, 11, 50, 141
world economy, 33, 35, 153
world-market, 31
world-system theory, 31, 35, 50
world trade, 32
Zambia, 136, 143
Zehr, Howard, 154
zero-order correlation, 40